10684790

FAITH IN A SECULAR AGE

DATE DUE

Harper ChapelBooks

KENNETH SCOTT LATOURETTE: Christianity Through the Ages CB1

HARRY EMERSON FOSDICK: On Being a Real Person CB2

ELTON TRUEBLOOD: The Common Ventures of Life: *Marriage, Birth, Work, Death* CB3

PAUL SCHERER: For We Have This Treasure CB4

HAROLD E. FEY: The Lord's Supper: *Seven Meanings: Memorial, Thanksgiving, Covenant, Affirmation, Spiritual Strength, Atonement, Immortality* CB5

MARGUERITTE HARMON BRO: More Than We Are. *New Revised Edition* CB7

HARRY EMERSON FOSDICK: The Man From Nazareth: *As His Contemporaries Saw Him* CB8

WILLIAM BARCLAY: Prayers For The Christian Year CB9

FREDERICK WARD KATES: A Moment Between Two Eternities CB10

ROBERT H. PFEIFFER: The Books of the Old Testament CB11

WALTER TROBISCH, Ed.: I Loved a Girl: *A Private Correspondence between Two Young Africans and their Pastor. Introduction by David R. Mace* CB12

AMERICAN ASSOCIATION OF SCHOOL ADMINISTRATORS: Religion in the Public Schools CB13

JOHN SUTHERLAND BONNELL: No Escape from Life CB14

ALICE PARMELEE: A Guidebook to the Bible CB15

DANIEL DAY WILLIAMS: God's Grace and Man's Hope: *An Interpretation of the Christian Life in History* CB17

ROGER HAZELTON: New Accents in Contemporary Theology CB18

HARRY EMERSON FOSDICK: The Secret of Victorious Living CB19

HARRY EMERSON FOSDICK: A Guide to Understanding the Bible CB20

GUNTER LANCZKOWSKI, Ed.: Sacred Writings: *A Guide to the Literature of Religions* CB21

GEORGE POTTS: Background to the Bible: *An Introduction* CB22

CARROLL A. WISE: Mental Health and the Bible: *How to Relate the Insights of the Bible to the Recent Findings of Psychology and Medicine* CB23

R. K. HARRISON: The Archaeology of the Old Testament CB24

FRANK S. MEAD: Who's Who in the Bible CB25

ALBERT C. OUTLER: Psychotherapy and the Christian Message CB26

WILLIAM BARCLAY: The Life of Jesus for Everyman CB27

COLIN WILLIAMS: Faith in a Secular Age CB28

LEONARD GRIFFITH: Encounters With Christ: *The Personal Ministry of Jesus* CB29

ROLAND DE CORNEILLE: Christians and Jews: *The Tragic Past and the Hopeful Future* CB30

BRUCE KENRICK: Come Out the Wilderness CB31

DANIEL DAY WILLIAMS: What Present-Day Theologians are Thinking CB32

HARRY EMERSON FOSDICK: The Living of These Days: *An Autobiography* CB33

EMMET FOX: Make Your Life Worth While CB34

GERALD KENNEDY: The Parables: *Sermons on the Stories Jesus Told* CB35

MARGARET K. HENRICHSEN: Seven Steeples CB36

ELTON TRUEBLOOD: The Predicament of Modern Man CB37

WILLIAM BARCLAY: In The Hands of God CB38

HAROLD BLAKE WALKER: Power to Manage Yourself CB39

ELISABETH ELLIOT: Through Gates of Splendor: *The Martyrdom of Five American Missionaries in the Ecuador Jungle. Illus.* CB101

261.8
W722f

Faith in a Secular Age

by
Colin Williams

H1288

Harper ▲ ChapelBooks
Harper & Row, Publishers, New York

TABOR COLLEGE LIBRARY
Hillsboro, Kansas 67063

JAN 6 '69

FAITH IN A SECULAR AGE

Copyright © Colin Williams, 1966.

Printed in the United States of America.

This book was originally published in 1966 by William Collins Sons, London, in the Fontana Books series, and is here reprinted by arrangement.

First Harper ChapelBook edition published 1966 by Harper & Row, Publishers, Incorporated
49 East 33rd Street
New York, N.Y. 10016.

This book is sold subject to the condition that it shall not, by way of trade, be lent, re-sold, hired out, or otherwise disposed of without the publisher's consent, in any form of binding or cover other than that in which it is published.

CONTENTS

INTRODUCTION   *page* 7

Chapter *I*   THE COMING OF THE SECULAR AGE   19
    Some Theological Interpreters
      Cornelius van Peursen   21
      Harvey Cox   24
      Arend Th. van Leeuwen   27

Chapter *II*   THE PROCESS OF SECULARIZATION   34
    1. *Thinking From Below*   39
    2. *Progressive Freedom From Ecclesiastical Control*   43
    Some Theologians of Secularization
      Karl Barth   47
      Dietrich Bonhoeffer   54
      Gerhard Ebeling   61

Chapter *III*   IS THE SECULAR SOCIETY VIABLE?   70
    Transcendence?   75
    1. *Eschatological Transcendence (Christ as Lord)*   79
    2. *Grace Transcendence (Christ as Saviour)*   84
    3. *Transcendence Over Death (Christ as Pantocrator)*   86
    Missionary Implications   89
    The Right Way to Reformation?   92

Chapter *IV*   EVANGELISM IN OUR DAY   104
    1. *New Openness to the World*   108
    2. *New Shapes of Missionary Obedience*   111

INDEX   123

INTRODUCTION

Does the church need to be radically re-formed? Is a significant revolt brewing inside the conservative structures of the churches? Is that revolt gaining enough ground to encourage liberals to feel that soon some of the radical reform for which they are looking will take place?

Can the church be freed from the sickness of its self-concern so that it will be free to join with the creative aspects of the radical changes now occurring in society? Can the church bring its structures up-to-date and turn to the tasks of working in our modern urban society for the truly human community we need and for the new style of human existence this urban society requires?

Can the church re-state its doctrine so that it makes sense in our secular society? Can the liturgy be re-shaped—not only its words, but its music and movements—so that it comes to life in the rhythms of to-day?

Questions such as these are stirring the ecclesiastical and theological waters to an increasing extent, and the ripples that are moving out into the world are creating some real interest amongst those who are dissociated from the church. The interest is mixed; a mixture of hope and scepticism. The scepticism is not surprising; past hopes have too often been mistaken. But there is no mistaking the hope that still persists; and the real question for the church is whether it can give this hope the encouragement it seeks.

In this book, an attempt is made to probe the direction in which the church must move if the hope is to be fulfilled. As one seeks to think about the vast changes that seem to be in store, the fears of the sceptics become easier to understand. Is it feasible to think of an ancient institution like the church, weighted down by its magnificent traditions, and with such huge investments in the passing social structures, managing to shake itself free to the extent needed to bring about a major revolution in a few short years? Or is it true, as the sceptics assert, that this is to look for the institutionally impossible; and that new life (if it is to come at all) must arise in new structures outside the old?

I can simply urge that we must not assume that the miracle cannot happen. Who would have thought a few years ago, that any of us would live to see the changes that even now are occurring within the Roman Catholic Church? The Christian faith speaks of true hope as that which arises beyond the death point of ordinary human hope: a resurrection hope. Christian history would seem to suggest that there have been times when incredible changes have occurred; and perhaps we may be at the beginning of another such period.

Just to mention some of the high points of the story of past changes—undoubtedly in over-simplified fashion.

1. In the period of the *primitive church,* the form of church life was rather flexible. About the only buildings it had for three centuries were the homes of its few affluent members; and, in general, the Christians were content to gather wherever the world gave them opportunity for worship, for witness and for service. They gathered in 'house churches', or in communities of alienation (catacombs), or amongst captive audiences ('in Caesar's household' with the slaves). They moved out along the trade routes seeking to gather witnessing groups at all major crossroads, and when Paul spoke of the church (in his letter to the Colossians) as being 'in every place' he did not mean that every village had a 'congregation', but that throughout the Roman world the signs of

witness to Christ as the Lord of the world had been raised. The structures of the church, as such, were somewhat *ad hoc*. Ever ready to plant cells of witness and service, they were ever ready too to occupy the limited space the world was prepared to give them and to fit church order to the conditions of the particular place.[1]

2. The first big change in the structures of the church came when the state, at the *time of Constantine,* decided to adopt the church and to give it the task of christianizing the whole of the culture. We can still feel something of the shudder that went through the church when the world asked for these vast major changes. Some were sure this was an invitation from the devil. For example, up until then Christians had been pacifists; and at least one reason for this was that soldiers had to say 'Caesar is Lord', whereas Christians could only say 'Christ is Lord'. But now they were being asked to give the church's blessing to the raising of the cross over the standard of battle. What is more, for three centuries they had been a minority persecuted group, witnessing to the power of the cross—to the power of patient love to overcome the hostility of the world. The very word for 'witness' was 'martyr'—witness and suffering were in their view inseparable. But suddenly now they were offered power and status and ease; and were asked to bless the whole of the world's life in the name of Christ. Surely that was a temptation of grave proportions. What should they do?

What they should have done is still argued! Some even speak of their acceptance of authority and power and status as the 'fall' of the church. But without second-guessing, let us simply describe what they did.

On the one hand, they accepted the invitation; deciding that if Christ is Lord of all life then they must accept

[1] See, e.g. Eduard Schweizer, *Church Order in the New Testament,* S.C.M. Press.

the opportunity to seek to witness to his Lordship in every part of the culture as a God-given opportunity. So the church with the simple *ad hoc* structures of a minority community which, like its Lord, had no place to lay its head, became the highly-structured 'established' church which matched *its structures* to those of the world, *its liturgy* to that of the Byzantine court ritual, and *its theology* to the need to give total systematic expression to the way of God, infusing the total life of the world.

But there is another side to the story. The other side is the rise of monasticism. If the church accepted the call to relate the Christian faith to the structures of the world, there also arose a movement expressing the truth that the Christian witness is still 'under the cross'. As a witness to the danger inherent in the temptation of power and riches and status, the monastics stripped themselves of wealth and position and power as a sign that the world can be saved only when those who have power exercise it as those who have it not, and when those who have wealth use it as those who are not possessed by it, and when those who have authority wield it not as those who lord it over their brothers but as those who would be the servants of all. The monasteries too had another role. In the mythology of that time the desert was the gathering place of the demons. There they gathered to plan their attack on the city; planning their take-over as 'principalities and powers'. And so the monasteries went to the desert. They were front-line troops to attack the devils on behalf of their brothers in the cities; they were the spiritual athletes seeking to put a ring of protection around those who were involved in the dangerous task of trying to christianise the world.

3. The third period can be marked with the rise of *the feudal period*. (I am tracing only the Western story. In the Eastern world it was quite different; a difference

we are only now discovering as the end of the centuries of separation from the 'Orthodox Churches' is bringing us into contact with this other side of the Christian heritage.) The rise of feudalism brought about the development of the settled village system. The old mobility was stopped; men were pinned down to the soil and ordered into villages. And again a major change in church structure resulted. The response to the new village system was the development of *the parish system,* with its village church and the local clergy tied to the parish. Because the whole of life now centred in the village, the church which was erected at the heart of each community became the centre from which Christian 'control' radiated out to all parts of life. The church ran education, health institutions, markets (setting prices, running craft guilds), and established the values by which life was controlled. Because the whole of life centred on residence, the resident congregation now became the basic institution of the church's life.

4. And so it has been for some thousand years, but with this exception. For the last hundred and fifty years—slowly at first, but now at breakneck speed—the world has been going through another revolution; a revolution as big as that which confronted the church at the time of Constantine or with the rise of feudalism. This revolution is *the rise of urban-technological society,* and the mark of it is that the feudal order with its relatively static life based on residence is giving way to a highly mobile world in which residence is separated from more and more areas of life—business, commerce, higher education, the world of health, leisure, mass communications. The church has been adjusting—a little here and a little there—by creating new 'boards and agencies'. But now the change has reached the point where the adjustment process will no longer do. Now we must face the re-formation need again.

What will the nature of the changes be this time? We are not sure yet; but we can say that major changes are already taking place. What we must do, is to try to make sense of those changes and to make a response now which will do for our day what the changes of Constantine's day and of the feudal period did for those periods.

Perhaps I can be excused a personal word, to give the background to what is written here. At the Third Assembly of the World Council of Churches in New Delhi, the Department of Studies in Evangelism was requested to undertake a study on 'The Missionary Structure of the Congregation'. At the time I was a Professor of Systematic Theology in Melbourne, Australia; but this study soon drew me out into the world of ecumenical bureaucracy, with the Department of Evangelism of the NCCC in the U.S.A. where this study had been accepted as the major focus of áttention. The study led also into the world of an expanding dialogue between theology and the social sciences, and down the road of the search for relevant forms of Christian 'presence'[2] in the urban-technological society of to-day.

[2] The word 'presence' has become an indispensable in-word in contemporary discussion on mission. It apparently came in through the French Jesuit missionary Charles de Foucauld with his belief that the common view, in which mission is seen primarily in verbal terms, needs to be replaced by a recognition that mission is first a 'being-there'—a servant presence in love on behalf of Christ—and that the opportunity to name the Name is one for which we must long, but which must know its right time. By now, 'presence' has become something of a code word and it may be wise to quote a current definition to show how it is being used. This one is from the 1964 General Committee Report of the World Student Christian Federation. After speaking of the 'way of life' of Jesus in terms of 'his identification with man, his humility, his form as a servant, his freedom, his interest in those who were cast out of society for either good or bad reasons', it continues:

'We use the word "presence" (*présence, presencia*) to describe this way of life. It does not mean that we are simply there; it tries to describe the adventure of being there in the name

It was not long before the fertile study process of the 'working groups' (appointed first in Europe and the U.S.A. and gradually in other regions of the world) gave rise to material which was clearly of real importance for the churches. If the study material—the work of a combination of theologians, social scientists, pastors and those experimenting in new forms—was on the right track, then it was rather obvious that the present structures of the churches would need to undergo major transformation if they were to develop a truly missionary relationship to the world. As the papers of these working groups were published[3] they quickly attracted attention in ecumenical circles; but no one would deny that these circles are rather restricted. So it soon was pointed out that a study book was needed to make this material

---

of Christ, often anonymously, listening before we speak, hoping that men will recognize Jesus for what he is and stay where they are involved in the fierce fight against all that dehumanizes, ready to act against demonic powers, to identify with the outcast, merciless in ridiculing modern idols and new myths. When we say "presence" we say that we have to get into the midst of things even when they frighten us. Once we are there, we may witness fearlessly to Christ if the occasion is given; we may also have to be silent. "Presence" for us means "engagement", involvement in the concrete structures of our society. It indicates a priority. First we have to be there before we can see our task clearly. In one sense of the word presence precedes witness. In another sense, presence is witness. For us presence spells death to the *status quo* both in society and in the Christian community: we will not tire of pleading and working for the restoration of normal manhood as we see it in Jesus. But our presence is not optimism. From what happened to the Lord, we know what resistance and opportunity to expect. And as for our weak faith, our poverty of understanding of what we believe, we trust that while present we will be given new words or authentic silence.'

[3] In *Concept*, published as occasional papers by the Department of Studies in Evangelism, World Council of Churches, Geneva, under the editorship of Hans Jochen Margull, the Director of the Department and the man responsible for the organization and supervision of the world-wide study process.

available to pastors and key laymen so that they could share in the process of rethinking. After all, it was they who would be most affected if a major transformation of the churches' relation to the world were to occur; and it was certainly unrealistic to assume that any such needed change could take place unless they were involved in the thinking that should lead to it.

The result was that in 1963 from the Department of Evangelism in the NCCC we published such a study book entitled *Where In The World?*, a title suggesting the questions: Where in the World *is* the church? and Where in the World *ought* it to be? No special publicity was given to it; instead we thought it better to allow for experimental study of it in church groups to which we had access. We were taken by surprise. The demand and interest far exceeded our expectations and we soon discovered that we were riding a wave of interest which we had done nothing to create, but which was now catching up our study and carrying it along. 'Renewal' was in the air; and who can count the contributing factors? Pope John XXIII, Vatican Council II and its talk of *aggiornamento* (modernizing); World Council of Churches' emphases on discovering the ministries of the laity and on the needed trinity of 'renewal, mission and unity'; the strong insistence emerging from Asia and Africa that changes were needed to move the church from being a predominantly Western institution to being a truly ecumenical body; the powerful pressures from the world of secular events, cracking apart the old social structures and raising questions as to whether God was in the whirlwind and as to whether the churches by their alignment with the old were themselves to suffer a smashing by the whirlwind. Our study found itself tossed along on the wave of interest developed by such forces.

In 1964 it seemed necessary to write a follow-up study book. *Where In The World?* had aroused great interest. Clearly there was a new mood moving across the face of the churches, focusing in the feeling that the time has come for the church to be released from its self-concern in order to find its life by becoming the servant body of Christ in the midst of the world with its fast changing needs and hopes and surging forces charged with incredibly creative and destructive potential. But *Where In The World?* had given rise also to serious doubts —clearly there was a new mood of anxiety developing as the shadow side of the new mood of search for change. Fears that destructive changes would undermine the effectiveness of present congregations; fears that the present church alliance with the family would be weakened by a precipitous rush to get the church out into the public areas of life; fears that theological anchors would be pulled up by the storm and that we would find ourselves adrift in the unsafe waters of a new Social Gospel; these fears came to the surface in the discussion on *Where In The World?*. This was the reason for the publication in 1964 of *What In The World?* which used the same study book format to speak to the anxieties that had surfaced in the course of the study. The new title was intended to point to the questions: What in the World should the church be doing? with the emphasis again, of course, on the world in which God is at work and for which the church exists.

In the meantime the study on 'The Missionary Structure of the Congregation' was being pursued in the regional 'working groups', and more and more it was becoming evident that behind the changes in the institutional relation of the church to the world there lies the deeper question of the changing relation of man to his world. If we were to fulfil the task given us of exploring the changes in institutional structure that are now needed, we could not avoid some exploration of this deeper dimension; a dimension perhaps best described as the change in man's 'mental structures' or in our way of thinking about our world; a change represented particularly by the rise of the secular society. In the working groups some attention has been given to this. But what is needed is that the work of our study should be related to the vast amount of work which philosophers, social scientists and theologians are now doing within this area.[4] These pages centre on that task. They are an attempt to begin relating what has been done in 'The Missionary Structure of the Congregation' study to some of the work being done in the exploration of the rise of the secular age.

In December 1964 to January 1965 I made a short visit back to Australia to give a series of lectures in a study course arranged by 'Frontier'—an ecumenical but independent body whose task is to explore the mission of the church on the emerging frontiers of secular life in that land 'down under'. In those lectures I took the opportunity for giving a preliminary report on the attempt to relate the structure study to the thinking about the secular age. The attempt was quite exploratory and undoubtedly lacked balance; but it was clear that the participants in the course believed that the area being explored is of crucial importance.

After returning to the U.S.A., I took up the study again when the occasion of Wieand Lectures at Bethany Theological Seminary in Chicago provided the opportunity to work towards a more balanced treatment of the subject. As the lectures developed, one feeling grew stronger— the feeling that the mystery of the Christian faith (and of life itself) is too profound for the capacities and

[4] In *What In The World?*, p. 49, I referred to the vast revolution in human attitudes to the world represented by 'secularization'; but added the footnote: 'In this Chapter no attempt is made to tackle the whole vast subject. All that is done is to look at some aspects of it which have thrust themselves into the present study.' I can now witness to the truth behind the suspicion, that once secularization thrusts itself in, it has a habit of taking over! Soon it became necessary to give it major attention; and now this book is the result.

categories we have for expressing it! Christians have always known that. 'We are no better than pots of earthenware to contain this treasure' (II Cor. 4.7), Paul reminds us; and as theologians throughout the centuries have sought to express the faith in the earthen vessels of our thinking, they have complained incessantly of the difficulties of the task. The vessels are not only too small; they are never the right shape! We work on remoulding the vessels of our thought to make them more suitable to carry the treasure of the gospel to our culture; only to find that just when we seem to be getting near it, the culture itself changes and we are forced to start shaping the vessels again. But there is no escaping the necessity for these ever new attempts; especially as the gospel itself is a major factor in bringing about changes in our culture. And so in each generation we struggle to use those earthen vessels to carry the treasure of the gospel to our culture, knowing that the next generation will see serious faults in our work just as clearly as we think we see faults in the work of our predecessors. But as Kierkegaard once reminded us (in his usual disconcerting fashion), 'our greatest comfort is in knowing that before God we are always in the wrong'. He was not condoning willing acquiescence in error, of course. He was simply reminding us that in our attempts to express the faith, as well as in our attempts to live it, we are justified by grace alone. We know that our best efforts will always fall short; but our comfort is in knowing that God uses our stumbling efforts, for they are all we have to offer and all he asks. 'We are no better than pots of earthenware to contain this treasure, and this proves that such transcendent power does not come from us, but is God's alone.'

In the original Australian lectures more practical suggestions were included, attempting to point in the direction of what this approach might mean for the relation of the churches to Australian life. For obvious reasons

these are omitted here. That is no loss, however. The
approach itself suggests that no one can do the practical
application for us in advance. This is the task for our
varied groups around the world ' each in its own place'.
'Everyone,' Luther once wrote, ' must write his own ten
commandments.'

CHAPTER ONE

THE COMING OF THE

SECULAR AGE

In the early stages of the 'Missionary Structure of the Congregation' study the primary focus of attention was on the problem of the institutional forms of the churches' life. The central question was how to transform or re-form the life of the churches so that Christians can be the presence of Christ at the focal points of modern society where our hopes and problems arise and where major decisions are being made or avoided. To put it another way; attention was focused on how we can celebrate our faith in God as the Lord of history, by joining him in his action in the events of our time as he moves toward the goal of 'gathering all things in heaven and earth alike into unity in Christ'.

At that stage in the study, the relation of the changes in the social structures of our time to the transformation that is occurring in our 'mental structures' inevitably arose; but without receiving any major attention.[1] Hans-Reudi Weber, at the meeting of the World Council of Churches' working group where a preliminary report on the study was drafted,[2] pointed to the need for relating these changes in mental structures to the changes

[1] See particularly *Where In The World?*, NCCC (U.S.A.), 1963, pp. 5off., where the problem of the rise of the secular attitude is discussed; and the article, ' An Interpretation of Secularization ', in the *Bulletin*, Division of Studies (World Council of Churches), vol. ix, no. 2, Autumn 1963.

[2] *Concept VII* includes that report. It is available from the World Council of Churches.

 41288

TABOR COLLEGE LIBRARY
Hillsboro, Kansas 67063

in social structures, and indicated the danger of theological distortion which would result from a failure to
explore that relationship.

Fortunately the nature of these changes is to-day the
subject of widespread investigation, so that we are able
to draw upon a rich store of writings. In fact the
riches are so great that anyone seeking to report on it
is constantly embarrassed by the ceaseless appearance of
new and important publications on the subject and by
the consequent difficulty of trying to state with any
feeling of confidence what, if any, are the emerging points
of consensus as to the nature of the changes in our ways
of thinking.

In these descriptions, however, there is one word that
occurs with regularity—secular. We are witnessing, so
the theme recurs, the rise of secular man. It is not
suggested that this secular attitude is the product of a
sudden change in man's way of thinking. On the contrary,
the change has been brewing for centuries and behind it
there lie factors such as the rise of the scientific attitude,
the successful bid for the autonomy of increasing areas
of human thought from ecclesiastical tutelage, the subsequent flight of institutions from the church's direct
control (with schools, hospitals and service institutions
forging their own independent life in freedom from mother
church), and the spread of an attitude of this-worldly
confidence in the ' second nature ' which is the work
of man's own creative hands. In turn, this feeling of new
confidence in expanding human creativity has served gradually to dissolve man's primitive sense of total dependence
on the ' first nature ' as the work of God's hands. With this
increasing dependence upon the new things that man can
create ' from below ', there has come also a continuing
diminution of the sense that God rules all things ' from
above ' through the wisdom that comes down into our
life through religion and revealed truth.

The slogan of the eighteenth century Enlightenment, 'Dare to be wise', is symbolic of this change. It is the announcement of man's desire and determination to think from below, through the wisdom that he himself can acquire through observation and exploration. From that day, man has increasingly thrown off the swaddling clothes of metaphysics and religious control—the secular society was on the way. In the words of Karl Jaspers, 'our world has lost its naïveté.'

This secular attitude, then, has been on the way for centuries, and yet it is only in our day that its hour has struck. Until now the ferment has been in the minds of the few, but now it is spreading to the masses throughout the world. That is why it is now possible for the first time to speak of the secular age, and that is also why writers are now exploring the significance of this vast change as a universal phenomenon that is spreading throughout our society. Our task in this book is to focus attention on what this vast change means for the church in its relation to the world.

A quick summary of three current attempts to state the meaning of that change will help us to see something of what is here at stake.

1. We turn first to a Dutch sociologist and lay theologian, *Cornelius van Peursen,* who has attempted to dramatize the significant changes that have occurred in man's thinking concerning his world, by picturing three periods of history, characterized by three contrasting attitudes.[3]

Period 1, van Peursen describes as *the period of myth;* a period in which the attitude to the world is one in which

[3] In *The Student World,* no. 1, 1963, there is an article in which van Peursen outlines these views. Harvey Cox, *The Secular City,* Macmillan, New York, 1965; particularly pp. 64ff., gives a summary that draws on further writings of van Peursen, as yet untranslated.

man as subject easily merges into the world of things. It is a period in which the world is rather like an enchanted forest, alive with magical and frightening forces, and in which primitive man makes no clear distinction between his life and the life forces permeating the world. In this period man sought to express his self-understanding by means of myths.

Period 2 he describes as *the ontological period,* in which man sought better control of his world by developing a rational understanding of it. Man was able to place himself in relation to his world. He did this by means of the concept of a chain or ladder of being. Above him on the ladder of being was the spiritual world, with God at the top as the source of being; and below him was the material world. Man in the middle position, received understanding from above him, and was in turn the source of rational control for the world beneath him. He thus gained increasing differentiation from his world and was able to gain the sense of security that comes from feeling that life is orderly and subject to rational control. All things were given their assigned place in a total order of understanding, and the relation of God to the world became more rational and less unpredictable.

Period 3, into which we are now entering, is called *the functional period,* in which the scaffolding of an all-embracing ontological understanding of life, now felt by man to be unnecessary, is being dismantled. Man's increasing confidence in his ability to understand and control the forces of life from below, is leading in turn to an attitude to the world in which man is prepared to live pragmatically, on the basis of the truths he discovers within his functioning world. ' The nouns of the ontological era become the verbs of the functional era. Now the concern is with thinking rather than with thought, with acting justly rather than with justice, and with " the art of loving " rather than with love.' He summarizes the change

by saying that 'in the period of myth, the main issue was
that something is; in the period of ontological thinking, it was *what* something is; in the period of functional
thinking, it is *how* something is, how it functions.'[4]

Van Peursen points to the fact that this pragmatic-
functional character of modern thinking faces Christians
with the major question : how does this square with
the biblical tradition? Does the biblical faith depend
upon mythical or ontological views of the world? Does
it mean that the coming of the functional era faces us
with the necessity of either opposing this modern way of
thinking in favour of the older views, or of abandoning
the biblical faith? It is his belief that it does not; and
that instead we now have the arduous task of learning
to read the Bible without metaphysical assumptions in
order that we may relate the biblical faith to the 'mental
structures' of contemporary man. As illustrations of what
this might mean, let us take just two words; God and
truth, and see how van Peursen sets about this re-reading
the Bible.

When we read the Bible without metaphysical assumptions, he says, we are free to see that the word 'God'
has no meaning in itself. It is a functional word that
acquires its meaning in history. In mythical or ontological
periods it acquires its content from the way in which man
thinks about his relation to the world; but in the functional period, this mythological or ontological content
dissolves. Now when we read the Bible in the light of
that fact, we gain a new understanding of why the
Jews were so hesitant to speak the name God. They
knew that the name does not stand for a separate thing
or an entity. God is known in his acts; and for that
reason the name God is truly a functional word given
its content in history. For that reason too, God is truly
known not in the world of rational abstraction, but

[4] Quoted in Cox, *op. cit.*, p. 65.

in the world of historical encounter. Myth and meta-physics are not his worlds; history is.

Likewise, the word 'truth' for the Hebrews refers to that which is dependable and reliable rather than to that which can be rationally placed in a system. God is true because he does what he says he will do. He is known as God therefore not in ontological categories that derive from our attempts to organize reality into a total system of understanding—in that framework the key ideas about God are omnipotence, omnipresence, omniscience—but in functional categories that describe his action—and in that framework God is known by what he does: 'He brought us up out of the land of Egypt, out of the house of bondage.'

For van Peursen then, the rise of secular thinking, rather than being an enemy which the biblical faith requires us to fight, is an opportunity for us to learn to read the story of the Bible with new eyes of under-standing—taking off the metaphysical spectacles which in the past provided the categories of understanding, and reading instead with the eyes of secular man.

2. The second attempt to explain the meaning of the rise of secular man is provided for us by an American theologian, *Harvey Cox*. In his book *The Secular City* Cox gives a somewhat parallel account of the changes in man's attitude to the world to that given by van Peursen. However, in a contrast which is characteristic of the difference in temper between the European and American attitudes, Cox replaces the philosophical categories used by van Peursen—mythical, ontological, functional—with sociological categories—tribe, town, city. In so doing Cox helps us to see the inseparable relation between the 'thought structures' and the 'social structures' of human existence and so helps to remind us of the necessity for holding the consideration of the two together as we

struggle with the question of the relation of the church to the contemporary world.

i. *The period of the tribe* corresponds with the period of myth. It is marked by the acceptance of close kinship ties as the basis for association. It is the period during which man moves ' from a belief in ghosts and demons to a belief in gods, from spells and incantations to prayers, from shamans and sorcerers to priests and teachers, from myth and magic to religion and theology.'[5]

ii. *The period of the town* succeeds that of the tribe and marks ' one of the decisive breakthroughs of human history.' People break through the limiting boundaries of kinship and 'form a new type of community, loyalty to whose laws and gods replaced the more elemental kinship ties which had previously held force.' It is in this period that the magical, mythical world gives way to the rational world of the ontological age.

In the period of the town, the attitude is still to some extent tribal. We are still far from a truly open world where man is free from the limitations not only of kinship ties, but of myths and ideologies that set groups over against each other. Each town still had its own provincial and limited loyalties. It is not until the rise of the third period that these limitations are in principle overcome.

iii. *The third period* is that *of the city* or technopolis. Here now we reach a form of society in which the basis on which men are brought together is functional rather than traditional. In principle the modern city is an open community which disregards tribal, or racial, or class or caste boundaries, and allows people to associate freely and openly on the basis of the functions they perform. There are of course strong resistances to this logic of the city; but the very reason why these resistances to the open community are so often irrational and fierce and so often take the ugly shapes of prejudice and hostility,

[5] Cox, *op. cit.*, p. 8.

is that they are resistances to the essential thrust of technological society.[6]

The character of thinking which the city ushers in is, as van Peursen noted, pragmatic or functional. Because of that it is not only ' open ' sociologically, it is also, in principle, open ideologically with man's thinking and understanding of life rising from within his experience of the world. It is in fact this openness which has resulted in the process of secularization, and man's turning away from the metaphysical thinking of the past in which he sought to place his understanding of this world within the wider ontological framework from which all truth was assumed to flow. Now man's dominant way of thinking is no longer one in which he seeks understanding of reality in terms of principles derived from ' outside '. Instead man's normal approach to understanding is to assume that he should investigate it with an open attitude from within the reality of this world. This development, writes Cox, ' implies a historical process, almost certainly irreversible, in which society and culture are delivered from tutelage to religious control and closed metaphysical world-views.'[7] It delivers man into increasing self-responsibility; to a relativization of values by the removal of the fixed metaphysical scaffolding; and to a desacralization of life by the removal of the authority of those who were assumed to be the arbiters of the pre-established system of values.

Again it may seem that this secularization should be seen as at enmity with the biblical viewpoint. But the thesis of Cox's book is that instead it is true that this secularization should be seen as the fruit of the biblical faith; and that, properly understood, the secular attitude is one which frees us to see something of the true dimen-

[6] We should not conclude, however, that because the opposition to the ' open ' community is irrational, it will soon pass away. The struggle against the irrational within us and around us is a struggle inseparable from our human existence—and from God's participation in it (the cross).

[7] Cox, *op. cit.*, p. 20.

sions of the biblical revelation of God as the living God who is known in the events of history. This is a point to which we shall return; but so that Cox and van Peursen be not misunderstood, we must emphasize that they are not suggesting that the ushering in of this third phase of history is an entrance upon a Messianic age—an arrival at the moment of historical fulfilment. Cox sees the process of secularization as a liberating process and as the opportunity for greater freedom; but as a process which also carries greater potential dangers. 'Secularization is not the Messiah. But neither is it the anti-Christ. It is rather a dangerous liberation; it raises the stakes, making it possible for man to increase the range of his freedom and responsibility and thus to deepen his maturation. At the same time it poses risks of a larger order than those it displaces.'[8]

What Cox believes is that in this process we should see God at work calling us to respond to the new possibilities for movement toward the goal of an open community of mature persons—a goal revealed in Christ. But it is also possible for us to respond in a wrong way to this process of secularization and to allow ourselves to become prisoners to a new limiting ideology, secularism, which arbitrarily restricts the dimensions of life. This secularism functions very much like a new religion and prevents its adherents from being open to see what God is doing in the events of our time, and from being ready to respond to his call to join him in the struggle to move toward the truly open and free society which he intends for us.

3. It is this need to see God at work in the events that

---

[8] Cox, *op. cit.*, p. 167. Cox's book underplays the equivocal character of historical development. The main aim of his book is to free us to see God at work in the secular. In concentrating on that task, he gives little attention to the New Testament teaching which sees the presence of God in history under the sign of the Cross.

have led to the open world of the modern city and to
understand how we are required to respond to the movement of God, that is at the heart of the analysis that
the third of our writers makes of the changes that have
led to the rise of the secular attitude of the modern
technocratic society. Our third writer is another Dutch-
man, a former missionary to Indonesia and now the
Director of the Church and World Institute in Holland,
Arend Th. van Leeuwen.[9]

The schematic analysis of the historical development
which van Leeuwen gives is rather more complicated than
that given by van Peursen or Cox. He abandons the
simple tri-partite format which is the favourite of so
many sermons, analyses of reality and schematizations
of history. Instead he speaks of two eras—the one out
of which we have come, *the ontocratic era*—and the one
into which we are moving, *the technocratic era*. However, the tri-partite pattern does not disappear, for van
Leeuwen sees three stages in the process in which the
way was prepared for the death of the old ontocratic
era and the birth of the new technocratic society.

The ontocratic era van Leeuwen describes as the period
of history which was born out of the Neolithic revolution
and gave rise to a variety of civilizations in various parts
of the world, but all bearing certain common characteristics.
Under the term ontocratic he includes features such as:
the apprehension of life as a cosmic totality, with the
structures of life being held together by an ultimately
religious viewpoint and with the various orders of society
given their sanction within the sacred unity of the cosmic
totality. It is this form of society that is now in the
last stages of dissolution. We are moving into a new
era in which this ontocratic form is giving way to a
technocratic pattern. The basic characteristic of this
change is the uprooting of the cornerstone of all human

[9] Arend Th. van Leeuwen, *Christianity in World History*,
Edinburgh House Press, 1964.

society up to this time: the cornerstone of religion. The new attitude to life in the technocratic society is one of liberation from the fetters of sacred tradition and the movement toward an open, secular, man-made order of life. The physicist, von Weizsäcker, described the change by saying that modern science and technology have taken the place previously occupied by religion and the church.

Again, like van Peursen and Cox, van Leeuwen insists that this rise of the secular society must not be looked upon negatively; as though Christianity were forced to support the cause of religion and the necessity for a sacred society. On the contrary, van Leeuwen sees the rise of the technocratic society as the outcome of the Judaeo-Christian tradition, and it is the influence of this tradition which he sees behind the three stages by which the old ontocratic society has been dissolved from within, so giving way to the emergence of the new technocratic order.

i. The Jewish theocracy of the Old Testament with its belief that God is the living Lord of history who demands that he be known as the reigning monarch in the midst of his people, was a belief that inevitably worked toward the dissolution of the fixed features of the cosmic totality in which the ontocratic understanding of life was set. The ontocratic pattern was characteristic of the societies surrounding Israel and she herself inevitably used its language and its symbols. The institutions of the surrounding ontocracies were all there—temple, altar, throne, kingship—all set within the cosmic symbolism suggesting their sacral connection with divine powers expressing themselves through this structure. But in Israel the awareness of God as the King who is at work in history, served to relativize this religious garb surrounding their human institutions. Israel used the mythical clothing, and was constantly tempted to be 'like the nations': accepting the ontocratic view in such a way as to forget that God is the free Lord at work in history, changing, judging,

promising, and calling his people to respond to him as
he leads them on toward the fulfilment of his purpose for
them. But always their faith in God as King worked
to call them back from this temptation. At the same
time also it tended to work out beyond the borders of
Israel dissolving the hold of the ontocratic pattern in
the minds of men. Finally in Christ, the destruction
of the mythical world-view of ontocracy is completed in
Israel. The fixed cosmic temple with its altar is destroyed
and replaced by Christ himself as the living free Lord
of history. And now this faith in Christ moves out from
Israel into the world of the nations, there to continue
its work of breaking the hold of the ontocratic pattern
over the minds of men.

ii. In the New Testament, of course, we only see the
victory over the ontocratic pattern pre-figured in Christ
and not yet realized in society. The second stage comes
when this faith moves out amongst the nations in the
growth of Christianity. In this process, as in Israel, we
see no easy victory, for the Christian church too is tempted
to be 'like the nations' and to lapse back into the
ontocratic world of myth and magic. But with all its
limitations, we see in the development of Christendom
the unfolding of many of the potentialities latent in the
coming of Christ—not least in the passage of faith in
the living God of history from the limited world of Israel
to the *oikumene,* that is, to the whole world. Christendom made use, like Israel, of many ontocratic forms—
sacral kingship, the orders of society said to be established by divine right, the system of thought held within
a cosmic metaphysical totality and providing divine authority to established norms. But again, the constant pressure
of the faith in Christ as the living free Lord of history
continued its work within Christendom, relativizing this
ontocratic garb and opening the way to that freedom and
mobility within human existence which Christ brings

as he leads us along the path to the fulfilment of the purpose for human existence he has revealed.

iii. The third stage in this process of the dissolution of the ontocratic society comes with the modern rise of the secular society, where man is freed from the hold of the old mythical, magical ways of thinking and so is able to venture forth on the liberating but dangerous path of secularization. This outcome is seen by van Leeuwen as the fruit of the biblical faith. He sees the present tendency among Christians to fight against secularization, therefore, as a fatal misunderstanding. And he sees the common suggestion that we require now a common front among the religions to resist the secular flood, as a particularly unfortunate manifestation of that misunderstanding. It represents the failure to see that the stripping away of the ontocratic garb with its religious view of life, is itself the work of the Christian faith. What is needed is a recognition that this stripping away of metaphysics and the sacral character of society constitutes a summons to us to be free for the living presence of God within the events of our time. It is a call to us to be free from the static limitations on man's obedience so often imposed by the ontocratic world-views, and to use that freedom by joining God in the midst of the action as he works in history, moving to the goal of a free and open society of mature persons in Christ.

Again, van Leeuwen does not suggest that this entrance upon the technocratic society is the entrance into the kingdom of God. He insists instead that we must resist all utopian interpretations. ' As the seeds grow, so the seeds of Satan grow among the rest. The kingdom of Christ and the kingdom of anti-Christ both have the ends of the earth and all the nations as their final goal.'[10] Nevertheless the understanding of Christ as the Lord of

[10] *Ibid.*, p. 407.

history requires us to see the technological revolution as the inescapable form in which the world is being confronted with the continuing work of Christ in history. 'Where the voice of Christ is understood, the technological revolution is conceived as history and not as process: as a series of continual human decisions and not as happening inevitably "in the course of nature"; in the light and the dark of the "latter days" and not as the final phase of the ultimate goal: under God's judgment and grace and not in bondage to sociological laws. Where the Gospel is believed, there is the truth accepted that here can be no returning to the age of "religion".'[11]

In van Leeuwen's analysis the attempt to see what God is doing in the midst of this change to the secular society, is clearly the heart of the issue. He seeks to interpret these historical developments in the light of the biblical understanding of God's lordship over history. He believes that the biblical faith requires us to see the story of the Bible as a story that is being continued in subsequent history; as a story working on towards its fulfilment, and working now through the collapse of the old ontocratic society and the rise of the new technocratic secular society. In the framework of this understanding he sees the new society filled with promise; but he also sees it as filled with grave dangers. For example, with von Weizsäcker he asks whether we must not see the rise of modern science in the light of the creation commandment to man to 'subdue the earth', and in the light of the promise of Christ that men shall do 'greater works' than he. He asks whether we are not forced to ask the 'blasphemous' question whether these 'greater works' of John 14.12 are the wonders of modern technics. If we are to risk a positive answer, we must also recognize that these wonders are filled with nihilistic tendencies. They offer an unprecedented power to subdue the earth, but at the same time they offer an unpre-

11 *Ibid.*, p. 409.

cedented opportunity for atheistic self-assertion. What we are called to recognize is that our Christian faith leads us to discern in this very encounter of creativity against nihilism the results of the preaching of the gospel. For this reason it is in the midst of this encounter that we must search for the secret of the meaning of the gospel for secularized man.

In these three analyses of the changes in the mental structures of modern life, we can see a general agreement which, if justified, is clearly of great significance for the church as it seeks to discover the forms of missionary obedience now required. All three suggest that the rise of the secular attitude to life must be interpreted positively as the fruit of the gospel and that religion must be seen not as the cause we are called to defend, but as the mythical, metaphysical, ontocratic clothing of our childhood that we must now learn to put off if we are to be free for true faith in the living God as he is working in the events of our time. All three equally agree that the positive interpretation of the rise of the secular society which sees it full of God-given promise also requires us to see that wherever the promise is, there also the dangers gather; and that therefore we should expect an intensification of conflict as we seek to fulfil, our missionary obedience—not an easy entrance into the kingdom of God but a heightened struggle to make way for the signs of the kingdom which God himself is bringing forth through these events.

This is the thesis which we have now to explore—probing its rise and testing its implications.

CHAPTER TWO

THE PROCESS OF

SECULARIZATION

It is a strange fact that the word secular, after a period in which it was something of an enemy word in the church, now bids fair to becoming something of a hero word. To discover why, we must trace a little of its history. The word itself comes from the Latin *saeculum,* meaning 'of this age' or 'related to this world'. It is a time word, referring to the world in its temporal aspect—the world of time; whereas the other Latin word for world, *mundus,* is a space word, referring to the world in its spatial aspect—the world of space.

It has been noted by many writers that these two words point to two different ways in which we apprehend our world, and that these contrasting ways have had a profound influence upon the attitudes to life that are characteristic of different peoples. It has been suggested[1] that for the Greeks the primary apprehension of the world was as space or location and that they therefore constructed a picture of life, or a world-view, that was primarily spatial in character. Thus, for example, they pictured this life as set against the framework of a 'ladder of being', with the true or underlying reality of life being derived from this metaphysical world that lay behind the moving world of time. For this Greek view, as a result, time was a problem; and the moving world of appearance

---

[1] See, e.g., T. Boman, *Hebrew Thought Compared With Greek,* S.C.M. Press, 1960. This is a typical treatment; but it is a stock-in-trade of theological writers, with many warnings against either-or conclusions.

had to be seen in the light of the solid world of being that lay behind it and gave it meaning. Truth and reality are timeless.

On the other hand, the Hebrews' primary apprehension of reality was in terms of time. Truth was something that happened. Reality was understood in the light of the events in which they believed that God had revealed himself to them as the Lord of history. Truth and reality then, are to be found in the living God who comes to us in the events of time. Space is important, but it is seen as the arena for the temporal story and as deriving its meaning from its relation to God's purpose for man in history.

This tension between the spatial and temporal views of reality can be treated carelessly and misleadingly, as though the supporter of one is obliged to become the enemy of the other. It can be used to suggest, for example, that for those who accept the ' temporal ' or ' historical ' view, life can be only understood as a moment by moment ' event ' in which meaning can only ' happen ', it cannot ' be '; and that any attempt therefore to project meaning into any kind of continuing (' static ') institutions, or laws, or doctrines, is a reversion to Greek spatial nature categories which is foreign to the dynamic historical character of the Hebrew-Christian view of life.

To develop such neat either-ors is to misuse the meaning of the tension. When theologians to-day find themselves fighting against the spatial images that have come to a dominant place in the theology and liturgy of the churches—' the God-up-there '—it is because they have seen that the dominance of these categories has obscured the dynamic historical character of the Christian faith, and that if believers are to be freed to see the living changing presence of God in the events of our time, the stranglehold of these spatial symbols must be broken. But this should not be taken to mean that Christians cannot use spatial symbols at all! Whàt is being in-

sisted is that space has to be understood in terms of time.
God is doing something on those mountains and hills
and in those streets, and our relation to the world
of space must derive from our obedience to God as he
works out his purpose with us within the framework of
the cosmos. To state that in another way : the dynamic
and static symbols are both necessary, but in the Hebrew
view the dynamic gives meaning to the static, whereas
in the Greek the static gave meaning to the dynamic.

An illustration of this is provided by the tension between
two motifs which the Roman Catholic scholar Leenhardt
discovers in the Old Testament :

i. The Abrahamic motif. Israel is to be free to move
away, like Abraham from Ur of the Chaldees, from all
past securities, systems, laws, so as to be free to move
out where God leads into uncharted territory.

ii. The Mosaic motif. Israel must also be ready for
her life to be given a definite shape so that the nations
will be able to recognize the way of God. For this
reason Israel is given its laws, its creed, its institutions.

These two motifs point to a tension; and in the life
of Israel there was a constant temptation for reliance
upon the system of laws, rites and institutions, to lead
the people to forget that Yahweh is still the living Lord
of history. Reliance upon the static led to blindness to the
dynamic character of their faith, so that the prophets
were forced to cry out against this conservative reliance
upon instituted ways. This did not mean, however, that
prophetic protest in the name of God's freedom led to
the destruction of the static spatial symbols. Instead
the struggle was to make sure that the spatial symbols
remained at the service of the temporal. The law,
the institutions and the creed are important. But they
must be understood as subservient to the understanding
of God's purpose for man that has been given to Israel
in history. The law is given to shape the life of the
people of Israel so that they can obey God in the

events of history; and for this reason the law is derived
from the purpose of God for man that God has revealed
in history. That is why the Ten Commandments are
not presented as timeless truths, but as truth revealed
in time; and that is why they begin with the reminder
of God's action in rescuing Israel from slavery and
starting them on a journey. 'I am the Lord your God,
who brought you out of the land of Egypt, out of the
house of bondage' (Exodus 20.2ff.). The purpose of
the Ten Commandments is to be seen as moulding a people
suitable to go with God on a pilgrimage through history.
The laws, like the institutions, have to serve that purpose. And because God is the living Lord, he can change
those institutions, restate the creed and renew the law,
calling the people again to go out like Abraham. In fact,
all this did happen in Christ.

The tension between the 'dynamic' apprehension of
life and the 'static' apprehension of reality does not
end, of course, with a victory for the former with the
coming of Christ and the spread of the Christian faith.
Initially in the Christian church there was a surge forward of the Hebrew view, since the Christian's primary
experience of the world was as history[2] and they thought
of themselves as caught up in the vital movement of
God's unfolding purpose for history that had broken
through in Jesus of Nazareth. But as the Christian faith
spread, the Greek view gradually gained a considerable
hold, especially after the church gained an important
place in the world after Constantine and began to think
of itself less as the pilgrim people of God and more as
the giver of order to society. The static institutional side
regained dominance over the dynamic temporal side.

This gradual victory of the spatial over the temporal
images is reflected in the meaning that was now given to
the time word 'secular'. The secular—having to do with

[2] See Cox, *op. cit.*, pp. 18ff. See also Carl Michalson, *The
Rationality of Faith*, Scribner and S.C.M. Press, 1963.

TABOR COLLEGE LIBRARY
HILLSBORO, KANSAS 67063

this world of time—began to denote something inferior
in contrast with the 'religious'—having to do with the
contemplation of the changeless world beyond time. The
secular priest became one who served those whose lives
were spent in the profane order, while the religious priest
was one who lived in detachment from this world of time
contemplating changeless truth in the sacred order. Thus
too when church-state agreements divided life into two
realms, the pope and the clergy served the spiritual world,
while the emperor and the laity served the temporal or
secular world.

In recent centuries, however, we have witnessed a re-
markable process of secularization in which more and
more of life has passed from the 'spiritual' order and
the control of the church to the secular order and the
control of the world and its agencies. Not surprisingly,
because of the medieval terminology, in which secular was
an inferior word, this process has met with fierce resistance
in the church—a resistance abetted of course by the fear
produced by the gradual loss of the institutional control of
the church over the world. But now we are seeing in
writers like van Peursen, Cox and van Leeuwen, a revolt
against the medieval terminology. The very secularization
which has been regarded as the enemy, is now interpreted
as the result of the Christian faith bringing about the
defeat of the Greek spatial view of reality which had gained
the upper hand in medieval Christendom. For these writers
'secular' (pointing to 'the world of time') becomes a
word to be rehabilitated—not as a saviour word, for
secularization as such certainly will not save the world;
but as a word that points to the world of time where
God is at work and where we are called to be free to
join him where the action is. The word secular stresses
the positive fact that for Christians the world of time
is of central importance. Because God is the Lord of
time, the world is experienced as history.

The significance of this process of secularization is seen more clearly when we point to two of its major characteristics :

1. *'Thinking from below' in contrast to the previous attitude of 'thinking from above'*

We have mentioned already various ways of describing the major change which has occurred in the attitude of man to the world : the change from magical, mythical, metaphysical or ontocratic ways of thinking to empirical, open, functional or technocratic ways of thinking.[8] In the older forms of man's awareness of his relation to his world, he tended to think from above. It was assumed

[8] Harvey Cox, *op. cit.*, pp. 21-36, has a most suggestive analysis of this process of secularization.

(a) He speaks of ' creation as the disenchantment of nature ' —the overcoming of the magical view of life. The biblical view of creation with its separation of nature from God plays an essential role in this disenchantment. Nature, instead of being continuous with the divine, is seen in the biblical view as being ruled by the divine; and man, instead of being absorbed within a total cosmic unity, is now seen as the free servant of God's relation to the world. As a result nature is neither his brother nor his god; it is instead the scene of his relation to the purpose of God.

(b) He speaks of ' exodus as the desacralization of politics ' —with the ancient sacral legitimation of political power being broken down by the belief of Israel that kings are subject to God and that when they flaunt his purpose they are subject to civil disobedience. In the Old Testament we see the constant danger of relapse into neosacral politics, and in Christian history too this danger often triumphs. Nevertheless the biblical awareness of God as the living Lord working out his purpose in such a way that all men and institutions are subject to it, remains as a threat to all such lapses.

(c) He speaks of ' the Sinai covenant as the deconsecration of values '—beginning with the prohibition against graven images, and with the recognition that Yahweh alone rules relativizing all human values and their representations. God is free; man must be free for God. We must have no other absolutes beside him.

that there is an eternal pattern to life and that our understanding of the various aspects of our daily life has to be drawn from that God-given structure of truth. So, for example, theology was regarded in the Middle Ages as the queen of the sciences with all the other sciences taking their starting-point from the revealed principles that she provided. The divine world was the world of the eternal surrounding this world. The real world is the metaphysical world beyond the substance that we can see ('meta-physics' means 'beyond substance') and the order of understanding is from the meta-physical to the physical.

On this level, the watershed of the process of secularization is the period of the Enlightenment with its critical attack upon the assumed domination of metaphysical first-principles. The slogan of Immanuel Kant, *sapere aude* ('dare to be wise'), was an affirmation of their belief that man must use his full ability to explore the meaning of the world from below. It was a revolt for the freedom of the secular from the sacred; a bid for freedom from the prison house of pre-established norms. It was a declaration of war against the 'religious' attitude which assumed that all of life has to be understood in terms of the religious forces that impinge upon our existence from the supernatural world outside and which demand that we submit to their absolute control. With this revolt of the secular came the rise of the sciences, expanding the understanding of life from within so that less and less does man resort to the 'religious' as the source for his understanding and the resource for his control of life.

With the expansion of the realm of science came the contraction of the world of religion. For a while 'apologetics'[4] was able to insist that at the ultimate points

---

[4] 'Apologetics' is the name given to attempts to defend the faith against attacks.

of life—at the source of meaning, at the place of guilt
and at the frontier of death—science could not provide the answers from below. At these points of crisis
we are still dependent upon answers from above, so
that here we are given windows into the world of religion.
But now less and less does this kind of apologetics
impress. Bonhoeffer expressed one of the reasons. If
God, he said, only appears at the extremities of life
where man is weak, and cannot be encountered in the
midst of life where man feels strong, man will soon
object. He will not be impressed by a God who waits till
man is cornered, but is of no normal earthly use. But
there is another reason as well why this apologetic line
has less and less appeal. Men have come to feel that
at least enough 'meaning' is available from below to
manage our daily affairs; that at least enough understanding of 'guilt' can arise from psychology to promise hope
for its control; and that if 'death' cannot finally be
overcome, this may be simply a fact to be accepted. In
the meantime we can only seek to improve our skill
in the battle to keep it at bay.[5]

It is in this context that we can understand the famous
statement of Nietzsche, now so widely used in contemporary
literature: 'God is dead.' This is not really a statement about the existence or non-existence of God. It
is an anthropological statement; that is, a statement
about man's self-awareness and his approach to his world.[6]
It is an affirmation that the old approach to life from above

[5] The spread of this attitude is one of the reasons why
writers speak of our time as 'post-religious'. So Philip Rieff
in *Freud: The Mind of the Moralist,* Anchor and Gollancz, p.
297, writes: 'By "post-religious", I mean an attitude so far
removed from ultimate concern that neither piety nor atheism
can appeal to it.' It is the attitude of living 'from below'.

[6] Carl Jung spoke of the death of God as a psychic fact of
our time, basing his judgment on his observation that the
Christian God-image was fading from his patients' dreams.

has been abandoned and that the old religious starting-point is dead.[7] In J. A. T. Robinson's language, the outside God-up-there whose metaphysical world constitutes the starting-point for understanding life, no longer provides the framework from which man's approach to life begins.[*] That approach has gone. Not only is physics no longer dependent on metaphysics. The range of science now has broadened until even 'religious experience' itself is understood from below by scientific analysis. The swaddling clothes of metaphysics—of thinking from above by dependence on outside principles—have been cast off. The building of human knowledge is now assumed to have reached the point where the old ontological scaffolding can be dismantled.[8]

[7] C. Wright Mills in an article in *The Nation,* 8th March 1958, makes the sociological judgment: 'As a social and as a personal force, religion has become a dependent variable. It does not originate, it reacts. It does not denounce; it adapts. It does not set forth new models of conduct and sensibility; it imitates.' In other words 'religion' is no longer a force invading life 'from above'.

[8] In philosophy to-day, the dominant schools seem to be those of the positivists, the process philosophers, the linguistic analysts, the existentialists; all of whom seek to philosophize without benefit of outside principles. This is not to say that 'metaphysics' cannot come back in another form. There are those who insist that we must not avoid the search for a total meaning of life. At least, they insist, we must relate the meanings derived from below to each other. We must also inter-relate time and space symbols to each other; or else we will be abandoned to the 'moment' with no meaning holding our lives together across the flow of time and with no meaning relating our lives to each other across the cosmos. Such a metaphysics however, is metaphysics from below, for it starts with the meanings that are discovered in history. Whereas in the old system physics was drawn from metaphysics, now metaphysics is projected from physics.

See page 123.

2. *Progressive freedom from ecclesiastical control*

If the first characteristic of secularization is 'thinking from below', a second flows inevitably from it. The revolt of the secular brings in its train a revolt against the institutional control exercised by the guardians of the sacred. Roger Bacon was a churchman; but he was able to gain freedom for his experimentation only by warding off the attempts of the church to maintain institutional and therefore metaphysical control over his life. And so from within the church itself there arose a revolt against the control of the church. As science gained its autonomy and broadened its scope to more and more facets of life, it brought with it the gradual removal of more and more institutions from the control of the church. Economic institutions (market, prices, interest rates), schools, hospitals, were gradually removed from the power of the clergy and the institutional control of the church. If man's way of thinking was more and more being conducted without benefit of metaphysical principles, his institutional life was more and more being conducted without benefit of clergy. Charles West summarizes this process of secularization as 'the withdrawal of thought and life from religious and finally also from metaphysical control, and the attempt to understand and live in those areas in the terms which they alone offer.'

As this chapter was being written, two newspaper stories appeared which illustrate this changed relation of the world to the institution of the church.

i. *The New York Times,* March 16, 1965, contained an account of a protest meeting held by students and faculty at St. John's University (a Roman Catholic University in New York) calling for greater academic freedom. Professor Joseph Gannon is reported as saying: 'The day of the omniscience of the clergy is ended. The

average college graduate knows more than the average
parish priest, and this applies to certain college administrators as well.' We see here that the protest was
not only on behalf of freedom from institutional clerical
control. Behind the claim for freedom from institutional
control is a protest against the theological control the
church has sought to exercise over the lives of men
by claiming the right to decide how they must act in life's
changing situations through the application of 'eternal
truths'—'eternal truths' of which the clergy are the
appointed guardians. So Professor Gannon continued:
'We've been too concerned with what Thomas Aquinas
thought about 500 years ago. What did St. Thomas know
about the pill?' Even more significant is the audience
reaction as recorded in *The Times*. 'At this allusion to
the birth-control pill, a gasp and a cheer swept through
the gymnasium. "This is too good to be true," a student
said exultantly.' In that reaction can be felt the growing
desire to throw off the role of theology as a metaphysic
which supplies the first principles by which society must
be governed and which must be applied from above to
the changing circumstances. If theology is to retain its
right to be heard, it must win that right in temporal
commerce with the knowledge that is constantly being
discovered from below.

It is the belief that this rejection is justified and that
the Christian faith does in fact encourage us to express
our theology within the open framework of secular thinking, that is giving rise to the many attempts to restate
the gospel in 'worldly' terms. So, for example, Gibson
Winter[9] uses the concept of 'reflection' to describe the
mode of theology that is appropriate to a secular age.
It is a mode in which the participants think not in terms
of bringing eternal truths down to a contemporary situation, but in terms of their participation in an historical
situation in which their Christian judgment *now* is made

[9] In his *The New Creation As Metropolis*, Macmillan, 1963.

by reflection on the facts of the present situation in the
light of two other moments in the historical process—
the *past* moment in history that came to its fulfilment
in Jesus and the *future* moment or goal of history to which
the event of Jesus points. This present reflection is itself
an historical event and requires us to maintain true openness to the possibility that as we encounter the present in
the light of all the new knowledge available to us, new
dimensions of our understanding of the past ' saving event '
and of the future goal will be opened to us. Here we
see theology trying to remove itself from a timeless
metaphysical mould and seeking to be secular, without
in any way abandoning the pivotal importance of the
particular historical event of the life, death and resurrection of Jesus of Nazareth, and without closing our eyes
to all the new dimensions of the future that this event
began to disclose.

ii. On the same day that the story of revolt at St. John's
appeared, there were also accounts of a swelling tide of
public reaction to the death of a clergyman, James Reeb,
as a ' martyr ' in the civil rights struggle in Alabama.
Others had died in that same cause—black and white—
without the tide of reaction rising nearly so high. Why?
Probably we see here a remnant of the religious aura
surrounding ' the man of God '; and therefore a striking
evidence of a survival of an element of the world of
' Christendom '. But it seems likely that there is another
factor involved—a sense of relief that the church (as
represented by the clergy) now is finding a relevant place
in the secular struggle. If this is true, this second incident
can also stand as evidence of a strong desire, often un-
expressed, for the Christian faith to break free from
its static categories and to be open in its response to
the changing forms of need and changing ways of thought.
What is longed for (and also feared) is a celebration of
the faith on the living altar of the world's needs in
such a way that the worship of the church is brought

out of the timeless world of Latin sounds and Gregorian rhythm and feudal institutions into the living world of contemporary history. In this sense James Reeb is a symbol of a minister becoming again a priest to his people; as one man pointing to a legitimate ministry of all men in and for the life of the world. The increasing presence of priests and nuns, clergy and rabbis in civil rights activities and demonstrations can be seen as a recognition of the need to move away from imprisonment in the static religious world in order to point to God's presence in contemporary events. The reaction of the laity so far to this new stance of the clerics has been confused. The sight of the 'religious' becoming 'secular' has brought forth a mingled reaction of hope and resentment. But it may well be that this movement of the clerics will provide a major impetus towards renewal, by leading the laity out of the narrowly 'religious' concern which they have come to assume as the province of the church, into the concern for God's present purpose in history.

We need to confess immediately that the death of metaphysics and religion (in the sense of a sacral world bringing to holy institutions, ideas and people an aura of timeless, supernatural authority) is far from complete; just as tribal and small town attitudes continue to survive in the city and magical and mythical remnants of thinking survive in the attitude of modern, functional, pragmatic man. Nevertheless, these survivals do not alter the fact that the dominant and the emerging attitude of modern man can now be seen as secular. For that reason it is important for us to come to a decision as to whether this attitude is to be welcomed as a fruit of the gospel or dealt with as an enemy. To help us to come to grips with that question, we now turn to three more theologians who have been at the centre of the attempt to explore what is involved : Barth, Bonhoeffer and Gerhard Ebeling; all of whom have interpreted the process of secularization in positive terms. Paul van Buren[10] speaks of their interpretation as 'kerygmatic' in the sense that they see behind this development the work of God, clearing away the 'religious' and freeing us to concentrate our attention on the work of God in the events of history.

Karl Barth. 'Barth was the first theologian,' wrote Bonhoeffer, 'and that remains his really great merit—to begin the critique of religion.'[11] And in his continuing comment he gives the clue to Barth's treatment of the problem. 'He brought the God of Jesus Christ into the field against religion, pneuma (spirit) against sarx (flesh).'

'Religion' is interpreted by Barth as man's reaching out towards God; as man's projection of his thoughts about God together with the cultic forms that inevitably build up around this religious upreach. This religiosity Barth sees as one of man's greatest temptations, for men are tempted to trust in this work of their own hands and to confer eternal significance upon it. The biblical faith warns us of their danger. It speaks of this religion as 'fleshly,' in the sense that it is the work of man's own hands and stands in opposition to God. Over against this religion stands 'faith' which has its origin in God's approach to us, and therefore can be described in biblical terms as 'spiritual'. This faith is spiritual in that it is free for God's approach, whereas religion is fleshly, because it interposes our thoughts and cult between ourselves and God.

We are freed from religion only when we see God as the 'wholly other' who is not at our disposal, but stands in judgment against our constant attempts to make ourselves

---

[10] Paul van Buren, *The Secular Meaning of the Gospel,* Macmillan, 1963.

[11] Dietrich Bonhoeffer, *Prisoner For God,* Macmillan, 1957, p. 148; Eng. ed. *Letters and Papers from Prison,* Fontana, 1953, p. 35. Wilfred Cantwell Smith, *The Meaning and End of Religion,* Mentor, 1964, traces the rise and use of the word 'religion' and the contemporary development of critiques against it.

independent of him by creating for ourselves a religion in which we can trust. It is in the light of this reality of God as the 'wholly other' that we must see the first commandment to have no other gods beside him; with the consequent prohibition of idolatry. It is in this light that we must see the constant prophetic battle against trust in religious forms: 'Your feasts, your burnt offerings, I hate, I despise.' ' O you who say, the temple, the temple, the temple of the Lord.' This prophetic word of judgment against religion has as its purpose the delivery of men from trust in the works of their own hands, into a faith relation to the living God of history which finds its fulfilment in the life of obedience: ' Let justice flow down like a mighty stream.' The prophets sought to deliver men from an idolatrous trust in their own religion with its shrines, both physical and mental, so that they could be delivered into faith with its trust in the living free God who comes to us in the moving events of history. Barth sees in Scripture (as well as in subsequent Christian history) a long battle of faith against religion. The battle comes to its climax and fulfilment in Christ, who breaks through the religious idolatries of Israel in order to expose men to a naked faith relation with the living God.[12]

Since the Sabbath was the centre of the religiosity of the Israel of Christ's day, the Sabbath became the centre of his attack on religion. In encounter after encounter he broke through the idolatrous trust in Sabbath observance to expose the fullness of God's continuing demands coming to us through the neighbour and so demanding the free response of living faith and obedience.[13] Similarly

[12] Barth has a major section in the *Church Dogmatics*, vol. I, part 2, pp. 280ff., entitled ' The Abolition of Religion'. This was a major theme too in the work which first made him famous—his commentary on Romans.
[13] See, e.g., the story in John 5 of the Sabbath encounter at the pool of Bethesda. Cultic obedience had obscured the demand faith should see in the needs of the world.

the place of the temple and the religious cult comes under the judgment of Christ, until at last the static temple as a sacred place is destroyed and in its stead Christ becomes the living temple, destroyed and raised up, with members joined to him as living stones. Faith knows that it is called into relation to the living Christ; we are to be members of the living Body of Christ involved with him in his work in the events of history. To be 'in Christ' then, is not a religious cultic matter; now the day has come when no holy mountain can be the place of true worship, for true worship is spiritual in the sense of being free to be with the living Christ, the Lord of history.

Faith then, is opposed to religion. Faith is spiritual in that it is freed for presence with the living Christ in the events of history; while religion is fleshly because it takes attention away from Christ's living demands and diverts it to sacred places and rites. We can see then that for Barth, the significance of speaking of God as wholly other is not that God is outside history. Rather it is an insistence upon God's full freedom from our attempts to imprison him in our religious practices; it is a protest against our attempts to 'place' God, or to 'domesticate' him in such a way that we are freed from the full rigour of his demands.

At first sight it may seem that Barth in speaking of God as 'wholly other' is running counter to the apparent demands of van Peursen, Cox and van Leeuwen that we should dismantle the old symbols of God's transcendence which put God outside our world. But here Barth is speaking of the transcendence of God not in terms of God being outside the world, but in the sense of his being outside our control and thus not available to our attempts to domesticate him. Barth insists on God's transcendence as against the immanent religion of men's hands with its cult and shrines; but he does not locate God in a metaphysical world outside

history and beyond the creation. In fact he is just as
opposed to this view of God as are our other writers. Barth's
insistence, like theirs, is that God is the God of history
and that his coming in Jesus proclaims the secularity of the
gospel.

This brings us to a strange fact : that the false form
of metaphysical transcendence (the God outside), which
was the main point of attack for our first group of
writers, and the trust in immanent religious cults and
shrines (religiosity in the world), which is Barth's main
point of attack, go hand in glove. It is belief in the
God of metaphysics, magic and myth whose presence
must be evoked from outside which leads to the irrepressible
tendency for man to locate his entry points and mark
them out as shrines and cult. But the transcendence of
the living God of history is not the transcendence of one
who is outside and whose presence needs to be evoked; it is
instead the transcendence of one who comes to us in
often unexpected ways in the events of our secular
life and therefore warns us against those shrines which
would divert our attention from the need for openness
to his unexpected approach.

God's transcendence, in the theology of Barth, is the
transcendence of our ' other ' who meets us in the midst
of life as our Lord; it is the transcendence of a Lord
who resists all our attempts to control him; but it is not
the transcendence of one whose home is in a separate
sphere outside our world.

For Barth, then the insistence upon God's transcendence
is an insistence upon the need for man to be free for
God as he encounters us as the Lord of history, just
as for van Peursen, Cox and van Leeuwen the insistence
upon the demolition of the old myths and metaphysics
which place God outside the world is also an insistence
upon freedom for God as he makes his demands upon
us in the events of history. They agree that ' religion '

in both senses—the immanent phenomena of religious practice and the outside symbols of a God whose realm is separate from the secular—is required to give way to 'faith' as response to God who comes to us as our 'other' in the moving events of history.

We can see now why Barth insists that the incarnation is an expression of the 'secularity' of the gospel. It means that we know God as the one who makes himself known to us in the everyday events of secular life. It was, in fact, this secularity of Jesus which puzzled the Scribes and Pharisees. They looked for a religious Messiah coming to them from the world of the temple and the cult; but instead he came as a lay figure in the secular world—the Man who in his care for others revealed that he came to give man a truly human existence within the full context of the world of creation.

There are, then, two aspects to Barth's attack on religion :

1. Against religion in terms of man's reaching out to God, with its production of cultic forms that crystallize around that religious practice and tempt man to trust in those forms.[14]

[14] This attack against religion bears many similarities to Paul's polemic against the law. Salvation 'in Christ' here is salvation from religion as the work of man's hands; just as salvation 'in Christ' is for St. Paul salvation from the law as the work of man in which he puts his trust. But just as St. Paul knew there was a right use of the law, must we not recognize too a right use of religion with its separate times and prayers, its sacraments and 'sacred' forms? Barth would agree that 'faith' makes use of such cultic practices; but I am sure he would resist the use of the analogy of the place of the law to restore 'religion' to an honoured place. Barth is even skittish about the place the church gives to 'sacraments' —particularly infant baptism. He warns us that the long period of Christendom has given rise to a dangerous development of sacred forms which offer us a too-easy assurance of God's presence. Similarly he is suspicious of any doctrine of the church in which God's continued presence is guaranteed by the continuity of order. True, there is in all this a parallel to Paul's attack on the law and it would seem that we could

2. Against religion in its tendency to separate out a piece of life and to designate that as religious over against the realm of the worldly; as the sacred over against the profane. The danger in making religion a separate realm lies not only in the idolatry that results in relation to the religious; it lies also in the fact that the non-religious realm is thus withdrawn from the full scrutiny of Christ's demands. It is no accident that so many social conservatives find in the sacred-secular separation a theology that peculiarly suits their determination to exempt the social structures they have inherited from any suggestion that God may be working in them calling for radical change. The ‘religious’ God is indeed convenient for the privileged and a relief for those that fear radical change.

Before we leave Barth, we must point to what seems to be an important difference in his assessment of the rise of the secular world from the other writers we have considered. So far we have noticed that he is at one with van Peursen, Cox and van Leeuwen in his attack on religion; but it would appear that when it comes to an evaluation of the positive significance of secularization, there they diverge. Barth sees the growing secular confidence of man in two ways:

(a) He sees man's growing at-homeness in the secular world and the dying of the old metaphysical systems as the death of the old separate religious world which

---

legitimately extend the parallel by saying that ‘religion’ as prayer, preaching, sacraments, is like the law, a schoolmaster to bring us to Christ. But Barth would still insist that the law is a term with a definite historical meaning in the life of Israel which can be purified in the light of Christ, whereas religion is a term which is not native to Israel's faith, and because of its historical associations, best abandoned. Prayer, preaching and the rites of the fellowship are best described not as religion, but in terms of our faith relation to the living Lord of history.

opens the way to a truer awareness of God as the creator
who has appointed us to have dominion over the earth
and as the redeemer who in Christ seeks to bring us
into a full participation in his Lordship over creation.
Just as the Christians of the first century were called
atheists because they depopulated the heavens by wor-
shipping only one—the God-made-man—so Christian faith
can be seen as opening the way to a truly secular attitude
in which the separate religious realm is destroyed and
Christ comes to us in history as the fullness of God's purpose for creation.

(b) He sees man's growing confidence in the secular as
in itself in danger of becoming a new religion, with
secularism becoming an idolatry closing man off from
the judgment of God as the 'wholly other' who stands
over against us in the judgment of the Cross and mocks
all our attempts to trust in the works of our own hands.

In both of these points Barth and the three younger men
agree : but the fact is that in the writing of Barth the
emphasis falls far more strongly on the second emphasis,
the danger of idolatry, whereas the younger men give
greater stress to the promise of God in the process of
secularization. Their direction of attention is to the question of how we can understand what Christ is doing in
the events of our time—how we discern his presence in the
revolutions of to-day and how this calls for our presence with him in these revolutions, struggling with him
for the hopes he is bringing to birth and against the
demonic forces that would seek to distort or destroy the
hopes he is offering to his children. In Barth, on the other
hand, the direction of attention is to the warning against
misreading the signs of God's presence—against the inveterate tendency of all of us to give religious sanction to our
ways of thought and our political ideologies and thus to
find ever new ways of exempting ourselves from God's
judgment.

Bonhoeffer accuses Barth of being so afraid of saying
what God is doing in our history for fear of idolatry,
that he finishes by lifting revelation above history and
by leaving us with no real guidance for the events of
our time. While Barth speaks of God as coming to us in
history, in practice the continuing presence of God is
too hidden to provide us with the guidance we need in
living the life of faith in the world of the secular. For
this reason he accuses Barth of 'revelational positivism':
i.e., he accuses him of teaching that the presence of
Christ is truly apparent only in the one narrow strip
of past revelation history, with the result that this knowledge of God's action is not released into the everyday
events of our continuing life. By warning so strongly
against the danger of domesticating God in particular
religious structures and by insisting so strongly on God's
judgment against all our idolatrous attempts to say 'Lo
here', 'Lo there', Barth fails to give us the help we
need in making the dangerous but necessary decisions
as to how Christ is calling us to be his servants in the
secular events of our time.

This brings us now to the views of Bonhoeffer, whose
fragmentary utterances in this area have had an incredibly
widespread influence.

Dietrich Bonhoeffer. In a letter to Eberhard Bethge written
in 1942 when he was on the way to the Vatican to
receive code instructions for his part in the anti-Hitler
coup, Bonhoeffer wrote: 'I feel the resistance growing
in me against all religiosity, sometimes reaching the level
of an instinctive horror. . . . But all the time I am forced
to think of God, of Christ, of genuineness, life, freedom,
charity—that matters for me. What causes uneasiness
is just the religious clothing.'[15] And again on April 30,
1944 he wrote, this time from prison:

[15] Eberhard Bethge, in his Alden-Tuthill Lectures on Bonhoeffer,
published in vol. li, no. 2, of the Chicago Theological Seminary
'Register', February 1961, p. 29 *and Papers*.

The Pauline question whether circumcision is a condition of justification is to-day, I consider, the question whether religion is a condition of salvation. Freedom from circumcision is at the same time freedom from religion. I often ask myself why a Christian instinct frequently draws me more to the religionless man than to the religious, by which I mean not with any intention of evangelizing them, but rather, I might almost say, in 'brotherhood'. While I often shrink with religious people from speaking of God by name—because that Name somehow seems to me here not to ring true, and I strike myself as rather dishonest (it is especially bad when others start talking in religious jargon : then I dry up completely and feel somehow oppressed and ill at ease)—with people who have no religion I am able on occasion to speak of God quite openly and as it were naturally. Religious people speak of God when human perception is (often just from laziness) at an end, or human resources fail : it is really always the *Deus ex machina* they call to their aid, either for the so-called solving of insoluble problems or as support in human failure—always, that is to say, helping out human weakness or at the borders of human existence. Of necessity, that can go on until men can, by their own strength, push those borders a little further, so that God becomes superfluous as a *Deus ex machina*.[16]

To be a Christian, Bonhoeffer is insisting, is not to be religious but to be truly human. But the real question then is : what is the measure of the truly human? Bonhoeffer criticizes Bultmann[17] for allowing the dimension of human existence to be reduced to less than the dimension revealed in Christ. He applied to him the criticism he made of

[16] Dietrich Bonhoeffer, *Prisoner for God*, pp. 123-4; Letters and Papers from Prison, pp. 92f.

[17] *Prisoner for God, p.* 147.; *Letters and Papers,* p. 94.

liberalism : ' It was the weak point of liberal theology
that it allowed the world to assign to Christ his place
in the world; in the dispute between the church and
the world it accepted the peace dictated by the world.'

To be truly human then means being open to the
full breadth of the human existence that Christ revealed.
But this introduces a further problem, for Bonhoeffer
knew that this Christian way demands real tension with
the way of the world; a tension revealed in the Cross of
Christ. And how can that tension be expressed without
the believer becoming in some way ' religious '?

In his early work *The Cost of Discipleship* he had
written : ' Discipleship means estrangement from the world;
and we forget the real joy and freedom which are
the outcome of a devout rule of life.' His central emphasis then was upon the need for our life to come
under the judgment of Christ's overwhelming demand,
and upon the need for a rigorous and planned dependence
upon God's grace necessary to free us from easy acquiescence in the selfishness of life in the world and to the
costliness of the life given to others. Hence the stress on
the value of a ' rule of life '. Later, from prison, he
criticizes the religiousness of his early work : ' I thought
I could acquire faith by trying to live a holy life or
something like it. . . . To-day I see the dangers of
this book '—the danger of religion creating a separate
holy world of its own and of preventing true openness
to the brother in the world. But though he criticizes
the religiousness, he still insists on the validity of the
major thesis of the book—the necessity for a recognition
of a deep tension with the ways of the world.

If there is to be a truly worldly Christianity—a truly
secular faith—behind it there must be a reliance upon
the grace of Christ who alone can make us free from
self-concern and free us for the true worldly life of
concern for others. And because this freedom is a costly

freedom, there is required a 'secret discipline' from which
a truly Christian style of life can arise in the midst
of commitment in the world. Bonhoeffer remained acutely
aware of the danger of false worldliness—of easy alliance
with current attitudes. This, of course, was the great
tragedy of the German church of his time; and the irony
was that it was the attempt to keep the church out
of the secular world of the state and inside the religious
world of the church which had resulted in its acquiescence
in the false worldly values of Hitlerism. And so Bonhoeffer looked for a relation to the world which was
religionless; in the sense that it would cut through this
sacred-secular dichotomy and would dispense with outward religiosity in order to free itself for the real world
of human existence—the secular world. But he knew that
this relation to the world also must be redemptive in its
commitment to the true and costly transcendence of God
expressed in Christ's life of complete self-giving—in the
suffering life of the One who was wholly ' for others '.

For Bonhoeffer then, a non-religious life—a secular life
—was the genuine life because it was the life revealed to
us in Christ. In Christ we see God not as the Omnipotent
one standing outside the world—that God is the God
of the religious world with its separate realms—but in
Christ we see God coming to us in weakness and suffering and allowing himself to be edged out of life on to
the cross. And it is here that God shows himself as
the one who is for us in history—Emmanuel—and as
the one who desires us to know him not in a separate
religious realm but as the one who comes to us by the
roadside in the daily affairs of life. Secularization can
be rightly interpreted as the fruit of the Incarnation,
for this coming of Christ into our secular life has shown
us that the only God has the world of creation as the
scene of his saving work. So it is that because of the
coming of Christ the deities of religion are dispersed;

there is no other God than the one who has come to us in Christ, and no other 'religion' than the truly human existence of Christ.

'Just as in Christ the reality of God entered into the reality of the world,' wrote Bonhoeffer,[18] 'so too is that which is Christian to be found only in that which is of the world : the supernatural only in the natural, the holy only in the profane.' He was fully aware that the church has resisted this secularization and has kept on fighting for a religious place in the midst of life; believing that in this way it was fighting for God's living space in the religious sphere. But to Bonhoeffer this was a fatal mistake. ' The attack by Christian apologetics upon the adulthood of the world I consider to be in the first place pointless, in the second place ignoble and in the third unchristian.'[19]

1. It is pointless. As secularization captures more and more areas of life, religion is driven back to the edges of human existence; its God becomes a God of the gaps, and the parson is kept for the inner private life and death, as religion is increasingly driven out of the world. This is pointless; for it will even prove difficult to keep religion on this basis as secular science continues its invasion of the inward life and its attack on death.

2. It is also ignoble to hold on to the religion of the gaps—it turns faith into a Canute-like figure ludicrously seeking to demonstrate its divine right by holding up its hand to the advancing tide of secularization and commanding it to stop.

3. It is unchristian, for any attempt to relate God to the special realm of the interior life cannot be accepted. The God revealed in Christ is the God of our whole life in history. He is the secular God; and we must learn to give a non-religious interpretation of Christianity.

[18] Dietrich Bonhoeffer, *Ethics,* S.C.M. Press, 1955, p. 65.
[19] *Prisoner for God*, p. 147; *Letters and Papers From Prison*, p. 108.

We must see God, then, not as a God who waits to come to us at the edges of our life in our weakness and extremity; we must see him as the Lord who comes to us in the midst of the secular life at the points of our confidence and strength as well as at the points of weakness, and bringing to us the truly human life which far transcends our ordinary life because it is a life that is wholly 'for others'. His concern in all this is summarized in some notes he put down as an outline for a projected book; one he rightly believed he would never write :

What do we mean by 'God'? Not in the first place an abstract belief in his omnipotence etc. That is not a genuine experience of God, but a partial extension of the world. Encounter with Jesus Christ, implying a complete orientation of human being in the experience of Jesus as the one whose only concern is for others. This concern of Jesus for others the experience of transcendence. This freedom from self, maintained to the point of death, the sole ground of his omnipotence, omniscience and ubiquity. Faith is a participation in this Being of Jesus (incarnation, cross and resurrection). Our relation to God is not a religious relationship to a supreme Being, absolute in power and goodness, which is a spurious concept-tion of transcendence, but a new life for others, through participation in the Being of God. The trans-cendent consists not in tasks beyond our scope and power, but in the nearest thou to hand. God in human form, not, as in other religions, in animal form —the monstrous, chaotic, remote and terrifying—nor yet in the Greek divine-human of autonomous man, but man existing for others, and hence the crucified. A life based on the transcendent.[20]

In all of this I have made no attempt to give a formal

[20] *Prisoner for God*, p. 179; *Letters and Papers*, p. 164f.

definition of what Bonhoeffer means by religion, preferring
to allow the context to suggest the somewhat indistinct
boundaries of Bonhoeffer's concept. Eberhard Bethge,
however, attempts a formulation, and as long as it is
not accepted as a final statement of what religion means
in this discussion—for the concept is in fact kaleidoscopic,
with moving boundaries and changing characteristics—
it should help us to gain the feel of what Bonhoeffer
and our other writers are talking about when they say that
religion must be cleared away to make room for the
non-religious interpretation of the gospel for which our
secularized age calls and toward which the Christian
faith itself has been leading us.

First, religion is *individualism*. It cultivates individualistic forms of inwardness. It takes the form
of asceticism or concepts of conversion which all
abandon the world to itself. . . .

Second, religión is *metaphysics*. Its transcendence
provides the completion which is felt necessary for
this world. God or the godly is the superstructure
for being. Thus it secures the escape the religious
desire wants to have. Religion inescapably leads into
thinking in two realms: reality must be completed
by the supranatural. . . .

Third, religion is admittedly a province of life, a
sector of the whole. . . . Driven out from one department after the other in dreadful secularization, it is
still alive in the more remote areas. Is that the
Christian God, dwelling in a dark and ever smaller
province?

Fourth, religion is the *deus ex machina* concept.
God must be there for providing answers, solutions,
and help. . . . It covers up actual godlessness with piety
and religiosity. . . .

Bonhoeffer holds that the time for religion is
essentially over. . . . Christians give proof every day

of this analysis because they are not able to make
more out of their religion than a nice little province
of their real life. . . .

But who is Jesus? . . . He is the man for others
against individualistic inwardness. He is the lonely
and forsaken without transcendent escape. He wor-
ships not in provinciality but in the midst of real
life. He, though longing for him, does not experience
the *deus ex machina.* Thus the time for religion might
have gone, but not the time for Jesus. . . .

Non-religious interpreting must do the opposite of
what religious interpretation is doing: not making
God the stopgap of our insufficiencies, not relating
the world in its misfits to a *deus ex machina,* but
respecting its adulthood.[21]

It is this task of 'non-religious interpreting' that is
being undertaken by a good many theologians to-day;
and one of the foremost of these is the German Lutheran
theologian, Gerhard Ebeling.[22]

Gerhard Ebeling. Ebeling has shown us the extent to
which the development of secularization has brought us
to the position where 'religious' or 'spiritual' talk of
God, inevitably becomes idolatrous talk—'worldly' in the
wrong sense. Here is a typical comment:

Christianity is constantly in danger of becoming pagan
precisely where it seeks to be most pious. . . . The
spiritual realm is then made into a world on its own,
a separate reality which passes by the world as it
really is, instead of engaging with it. . . . Could it be
that separatist, unworldly talk of God which builds

[21] Bethge, *op. cit.,* pp. 33-4.
[22] See particularly Gerhard Ebeling, *Word and Faith,* Fortress
Press, and S.C.M. Press, 1963, in such essays as 'The Non-religious
Interpretation of Biblical Concepts', pp. 98ff.; 'Dietrich Bonhoeffer', pp. 282ff.; 'Worldly Talk of God', pp. 354ff.

a world apart is likewise worldly talk of God in that negative, basically godless sense?

It is indeed! The extreme possibilities of separation join hands: atheistic and, as it were, purely religious, purely spiritual talk of God. Both leave the world without God and God without the world.[23]

The practical importance of this issue in the relation of the church to the world can be illustrated from an editorial in the conservative religious journal, *Christianity To-day*:[24]

As a spiritual body, the Church has a message primarily for the spiritual needs of mankind. Once she shifts her emphasis from spiritual to secular matters her influence wanes; and this is the danger she faces to-day. In the New Testament we find our Lord and the Apostles living in the midst of social, economic and political evils as great as any in our times; yet we find their ministries primarily directed to the spiritual needs of mankind and we are assured that only as the hearts of men are changed can these evils be eliminated. However competent or informed the corporate Church may be or become in social, economic or political affairs, these matters are beyond her proper, God-given jurisdiction. . . .

So long as the Church interprets Scripture correctly, the Church will be kept from error. But when she becomes involved in a secular, controversial issue, those who oppose the Church's position on this issue will question the ability of the Church to speak authoritatively on ecclesiastical and spiritual subjects.

This is an incredibly clear illustration of how the separation of life into two realms—the 'spiritual' as the province of the church and the 'secular' which

[23] *Ibid.*, p. 358.
[24] The issue of July 17, 1964. An editorial signed by Harold John Ockenga, Chairman; and Carl F. H. Henry, Editor.

must remain in the world outside the church—results in divorcing the secular world from any real theological concern. Here we see illustrated Ebeling's assertion that ' the extreme possibilities of separation join hands : atheistic and, as it were, purely religious, purely spiritual talk of God. Both leave the world without God and God without the world.' It was against such a separation in Germany—abstracting Hitler's activities in the ' secular ' realm from the church's ' spiritual ' task—that Bonhoeffer had to fight. It is no accident again, that in our time there is a close correlation between this conservative cling-ing to the two realms religious attitude and right wing political viewpoints which fight vehemently against any calls for significant change in the racial, caste, class and political structures inherited from the past. To think of God as involved in the arena of these secular affairs struggling to overcome the patterns of inherited injustice and working toward the fulfilment of his pur-poses, is apparently abhorrent. God is isolated into his religion arena and the result is that the secular is without God and without hope—except, of course, for those who are already the possessors of secular privilege.

An historical note about the two realms theory may throw some light on this position. After the church was adopted by the state, Western Europe in time began to think of itself as a Christian culture in which the whole of life was subject to the Lordship of Christ. For the proper exercise of this one government of God, their belief had it, a working partnership had been provided. The two partners in this one government were church and state; each with a realm of life for which they were responsible. On its side, the church was to rule in the ' spiritual ' realm, with its weapon the Word and its concern being to bring God's grace to all men. On its side, the state was to rule in the ' secular ' realm, with its weapon the sword and its concern being to keep God's justice among all men. Both arms are needed for

God's government, and each must work in co-operation
with the other. Both are direct ministries of God; and
while the church should not interfere in the government
of the 'secular' it certainly must interpret God's will
for the secular and so train the rulers for their task.
Theology was the queen of the sciences. The secular
world was understood in the light of the wisdom flowing
down from the metaphysical world and received by the
rulers from the 'spiritual' realm from which they received their guidance.

We have seen some of the vast changes that have
destroyed the very basis of this two realms agreement.
The secular has been withdrawn from the metaphysical
and as a result more and more areas of life have been
withdrawn from the church's control and from the guidance
of theology. The only result therefore of continuing the
two realms thinking now, is that the religious realm to
which the church is restricted becomes a more and more
confined segment isolated on the edge of life, while the
secular becomes more and more separated from the judgment of God—an autonomous realm : ' the world without
God and God without the world.'

The conclusion of Ebeling—in agreement with the other
theologians on whom we have been drawing—is that the
breakdown of 'Christendom' and its two realm agreement, together with the increasing secularization of life,
are to be understood as the result of the work of Christ
in history. These developments are forcing us to see
that 'all talk of God is worldly talk of God,'[25] and that
' life in this world is the proper exercise ground of worldly
talk of God.'

Something of the practical significance of this for
the missionary relationship of the church to the world
can be suggested, although here only in passing, for
we will postpone a fuller examination until we have

[25] Ebeling, *op. cit.*, p. 359.

looked at some of the apparent difficulties in this non-religious, secular, worldly interpretation of the Christian life.

1. *Sociologically*, we can see how the two realms attitude has separated religion from the new ' worlds ' that have arisen since the development of modern science and within the secularist attitude—the worlds of business, industry, mass communications, modern education, leisure, health. Being separated from the religious realm the church has made only fragmentary attempts to find a creative relation to them. Instead it has been largely content to keep religion in relation to the home—the ' private world ' as against the ' public world '. With the rise of this secular theology however, we are now witnessing a strong and developing attempt to discover how the church can be properly present in these new worlds, and how she can develop legitimate ministries to public life in which the appropriate witness is given to the purpose of Christ and his continuing presence in the events of history.[26]

2. *Theologically*, we must see the need for a strong warning concerning the form that this missionary presence in the public worlds should take. There is a grave danger that the churches will try to return to their Christendom role by attempting to restore institutional and meta-physical mastery over the world. But ' it must not be so among you.'[27] This temptation to lord it over society instead of being the self-effacing servant of God's purpose for society is at least one good reason for that form of institutional separation between church and state which will enable the world to fight off the inveterate tendency of the church to aspire to the position of being the institutional viceroy of God. The church must learn

[26] This problem has received considerable attention in the World Council of Churches' study on The Missionary Structure of the Congregation, and is a central issue in the two books in which I have reported on the study.

[27] Mark 10.43.

now to see itself as the witness to God's purpose in the world but not as the controller of that purpose. Secularization must not be reversed; we must fight for an open society precisely because we believe that it is through such freedom that Christ is working toward the fulfilment of his purpose for history.

The situation facing the writers of the American Constitution is here instructive. From what I understand, their separation of church and state was not devised to split life into two realms—sacred for the church and secular for the state. That life too was 'under God',[28] and they were not seeking to establish a sacred-secular dichotomy. What they were seeking to do was to defend the world against the church as a claimant for institutional control over society. They knew from the long European experience, that as an institution under the control of ecclesiastics the church showed all the same tendencies to imperialism as any other institution. Therefore the same protection against imperialism which was provided by the separation of executive, legislative and judiciary, was provided also by the separation of the church and the state. The church, which for centuries had occupied the position of norm-setter, religious director and value maker for society would not easily surrender its pretensions. But the fathers of the Constitution believed that freedom from the Christendom position of the church was itself God given, and that therefore they must protect society against the return of the church to power.

As Christians we should support this insight and fight for an open society; and we must see the removal of this position of open authority over the world as the work of Christ bringing the church back to the right position in which to fulfil its servant role after the example of her Lord.

[28] The phrase itself, 'under God', is a recent insertion into the 'pledge of allegiance', but it is consistent with the viewpoint of the fathers of the Constitution.

According to the German sociologist, von Oppen, society itself is now moving towards a form that is potentially more amenable to this Christian insight. He speaks of the way in which the form of society based on 'order' is giving way to a form of society based instead on 'organization'. The society based on order was relatively static, religiously sanctioned and total in its scope. The society based on organization is one which is flexible, secularized, with a multiplicity of organizations of free association and limited claims. It resists the totalitarian claims of any institution (including the church) to be the source of meaning and the norm-setter or controller of society. It insists instead that creativity emerges best in an open society and that organization must be seen as arising freely to fulfil immediate functions emerging from open exploration; organization which must also be changed freely when experimentation points to improved methods of creativity.

Von Oppen believes that the emergence of this organization principle came through the Christian gospel. Its roots he sees in the insistence of the Christian faith on personal decisions and responsibility (rather than acquiescence in imposed decisions), and in the Christian emphasis upon the movement of God's purpose towards an open community based not on clan, or race, or nation, or any pre-established form, but on the free decision of faith. This tender shoot planted in history so long ago has grown slowly, and it is still and will continue to be subject to strong opposition. But the church must see in this tendency towards the open society a movement in line with its mission. It must see this development as calling for its participation—seeking to preserve this openness and creativity of the secular world with the potential it offers for true community. It must see in this development, too, the need for renouncing any desire on its own part to return to the old hegemony of a religious world, in the same way as it reminds us of the need to join in the struggle against all the new contenders for ideological hegemony.[29]

The missionary approach which these points suggest will require, of course, a considerable revision of the inherited patterns of theological formulation and liturgical order as well as the discovery of new forms of missionary presence in the world. It is encouraging to see that this revision is occurring; and not just in one denomination or geographical area, but across the broad spectrum of the Christian church. We take just one example; this one from a Roman Catholic source.[30] The introduction to the book speaks of the new theological approach now required in this secular age.[31]

It is difficult to sketch even in outline the distinguishing marks of this new theology. Quite clearly, however, it is deliberately based on Scripture and the history of salvation. At the same time it has the humble courage to confront the new problems arising from the human condition of to-day. It seeks, on the basis of our contemporary situation, a better understanding of the Word of God for man and the world in our time. A theological insight of this kind is necessary for anyone who, acting in faith, is actively engaged in the church and in the world.

At a time when the world has lost its reference to God and is fully experienced as a *world* in its earthly meaning, at a time, furthermore, when man is represented as a *faber suiipsus* who tries to interpret the world, inquiring about his own meaning, in a purely human sense (giving it a philosophical, technical or poetic meaning), the study of dogma is induced to concentrate with greater intensity on its own peculiar task, which is to bring out the near-

[29] Cox, *op. cit.*, pp. 175ff.

[30] *The Church and Mankind* (Concilium; theology in the age of renewal: Dogma, vol. i), Karl Rahner and Edward Schillebeeckx (eds.), Paulist Press, Glen Rock, New Jersey, 1965.

[31] *Ibid.*, p. 2 and p. 6.

ness of the divine *mysterium* in human life and the
implications of this for our lives as men co-existing
with our fellows in this world. For in the definitive
gift of himself in Jesus Christ through the Spirit,
God has made this nearness accessible to us in
faith, love and hope, and has made it livable in
practice in the *mysterium* of the church.

CHAPTER THREE

IS THE SECULAR SOCIETY

VIABLE?

T. S. Eliot in his book *The Idea of A Christian Society,*
published at the time when World War II was breaking
out, put forward the thesis that only a renewal of
Christian culture could rescue our society. Secularization, he believed, is ultimately destructive. A society that
does not find its coherence in established religious norms
cannot survive. A neutral society is not viable, for neutral-
ity simply creates a vacuum into which conflicting ideologies will run, battling for supremacy. Society must be
seen as a battlefield for the gods; and if the church
does not claim the field for Christ, its rightful Lord,
then it simply opens the way to the triumph of pagan
ideologies. The alternative is either a new Christendom
or the victory of the pagan ideologies such as Nazism or
Communism or their successors.

'It is my contention,' Eliot wrote, 'that we have to-day
a culture which is still mainly negative, but which, so
far as it is still positive, is still Christian. I do not think
that it can remain negative, because a negative culture
has ceased to be efficient in a world where economic and
spiritual forces are proving the efficiency of cultures which
even when pagan, are positive; and I believe the choice
before us is between the formation of a new Christian
culture and the acceptance of a pagan one.'[1]

The fear of the vacuum created by secularization and
the belief that a religious faith must always be the

[1] T. S. Eliot, *The Idea of a Christian Society,* Faber &
Faber, p. 13.

necessary ideological cement that will hold society together is a view that is widespread. It is assumed that either true religion will perform this ideological function, or else false religion will capture the field. It is this belief that we are in the midst of an ultimately religious battle which gives such popularity to that standard sermon which calls on us to exorcise the threefold demon— communism, materialism, secularism—which is said to threaten us with pagan control over culture; and which demands that, if we are to save our Western way of life, we must restore the Christian religious values which made our culture great.

The theologians of secularization protest. Such an attitude not only gives rise to a dangerous form of Western self-righteousness and to repressive games of ideological demon-hunting; it also fails to maintain that openness to the creativity of life to which God calls. It fails to recognize that it is this open attitude which, having been unveiled in Christ, has worked its hidden way in history and now is leading to the collapse of the old sacral societies. The task then, is not a return to the days of a religious ideology whose task was to hold society together. Instead we need now an eagle-eyed movement into a truly open society, ready for all the surprises springing forth from the world of human creativity, but ready too for the struggle against the demonic forces that threaten to destroy that creativity; thus blocking the way toward the ultimate goal revealed in Christ— an open society of free men whose full creativity is at last released by the power of the Spirit.

The case for this secular view is given in a direct reply to T. S. Eliot by Denis Munby in his book *The Idea of a Secular Society*.[2] He argues that time is proving wrong the claim of T. S. Eliot that if culture is not

[2] Denis Munby, *The Idea of a Secular Society*, Oxford University Press, 1963. See the discussion of this issue in *What In The World?*, pp. 55-6.

directly subsumed under Christ by the establishment of
the Christian faith as the norm-setter, then necessarily
some other ideology must move into the vacuum. Instead,
says Munby, the open, neutral, secular society is now
proving remarkably flexible and creative. It is proving
its viability over against those societies which seek stability
in an established system of metaphysical norms—as in
the communist countries and in the remaining parts of
Christendom. This strength of the secular society, says
Munby, should lead us to rejoice. To the traditionalist,
this secularization seems to be the banishment of God.
And it is the banishment of the outside God who main-
tains metaphysical control over history by the imposition
of pre-established norms to which society must submit.
But Munby's argument is that it is precisely abolition of
such systems of pre-established norms, with the adoption
of an open attitude to life, that is responsible for the
release of previously undreamed of creativity. It is also
enabling us to see that the God who has shown himself
in Christ to be truly free for man, is also the God who
desires us to seek his presence in the changing scene
of history—in the openness of the secular rather than
in the static timeless world of the religious. By this
secularist revolt of our time we are being freed from
static ways of thought, static views of society and static
forms of the church. The freedom of an open society
should be seen as a gift of Christ; as a coming of age,
with all the promise and trials that coming of age brings.
The task of the Christian is to struggle for the maintenance of this freedom, not to fight for a return to
Christendom. He is called to see it as an opportunity to
join Christ in his continued struggle in history as he
leads us toward the goal he has revealed.

In all of this Munby is appealing to the particular
form of Christ's presence in history. Christ came as
the humble one into an open world; not as an authority

imposed from above. He came not as the revealer of an ideological system superimposed on society, but as the one who in the way he gave himself affirmed the need for human freedom and decision. He came as the one who was prepared to risk his truth (and life) within the openness of the secular world. When asked to identify himself openly, by displaying his authority or by giving a sign that would convince man by its supernatural power, he refused. He had to be found, freely, within the openness of the secular world or not at all. This means that those who follow him should not seek to impose the Christian faith as a metaphysical formula or as a religious or institutional means for providing society with stability and unity. We should seek to maintain instead an open secular world in which we claim no established rights over other views, but in which we accept the responsibility to witness for Christ by seeking to point to his presence as he works within history; knowing, however, that as we seek to point, the surprising is what we must learn to expect.

This openness requires a readiness to recognize both the creative and destructive forces surging in history. A truly secular attitude must not be thought to imply an optimistic view of life; for wherever creativity arises, there also destructive forces lie close at hand. This means that the responsibility to seek to witness by pointing to Christ's surprising presence in the events of our time, carries with it also the responsibility to be ready for the struggle against the forces that always gather in opposition to him.

It should quickly be added that the destructive forces are not only those around us in the area of social problems. They also lie deep within us, so that the struggle is at once within and without. In his suggestive book *Life Against Death*[8] in which he attempts to explore ' the

[8] Vintage Books, 1959; Routledge, 1959.

psychoanalytical meaning of history', Norman O. Brown points an insistent finger at the truth in the suggestion of Freud, Nietzsche and others that we must understand history as 'an ever increasing neurosis'. In this suggestion he sees a psychological equivalent of the traditional doctrine of original sin. In it too lies a warning against the easy optimism which would conclude that the development of an increasingly open society with the gradual collapse of old caste, class, race and colour barriers, is leading to an era in which all such conflicts will disappear. Far from it. Brown quotes Freud's conclusion from *Civilization and Its Discontents.* 'If civilization is an inevitable course of development from the group of the family to the group of humanity as a whole, then an intensification of the sense of guilt . . . will be inextricably bound up with it, until perhaps the sense of guilt may swell to a magnitude that individuals can hardly support.'[4] The reality of this 'neurosis' (so tragically apparent in the present battle against race justice; but weaving its pattern in all of our inter-relationships) points to the relevance of the claim that only radical repentance, and conversion through the renewing power of grace, can open the way to personal and corporate health. It points too to the importance of what is called, later in this chapter, 'grace transcendence'.[5] Nor should we be over-optimistic concerning our readiness to confess our sin (admit our 'neurosis'), to expose ourselves to the healing power of grace, and to join in the action needed in society to overcome the destructive forces unleashed by our neurotic behaviour. The victories that come, come only through painful struggle—only by way of the cross.

Another danger we should recognize in this 'world come of age' is that while an open 'secular' world has been shown to be viable, there is still the danger of new ideologies emerging to seek to lord it over us and rob

[4] *Ibid.*, p. 15.   [5] See below, p. 84.

us of our freedom. Not the least danger at this point is that secularization will be turned into an ideology by becoming a 'secularism' that 'clips the wings of emancipation'[6] by holding life within the limits bounded by the contemporary range of our rational explorations.

TRANSCENDENCE?

A major problem posed by this 'secularism' and by the attempt to live from below without outside 'principles' can be put in the form of a question. We can put it this way: Is there a transcendent dimension to life? If we live only by the knowledge that comes to us in time, is there some way in which there breaks through to us in time a revelation of meaning that transcends the flow of time? Or are we prisoners of time, condemned to play a Sartrean game of trying to project some meaning for ourselves? To put the question in still another way: Is there some way in which the ultimate meaning of history has come to us within the stream of history; or do we instead simply throw out our own meaning as we are carried along in the stream, knowing that they will fall back, but knowing too that as we swim along these hypothetical lines can at least provide interesting paths for us to follow during the short time that elapses before they drop back into the stream? And to add another dimension to the question; in view of the destructive forces that constantly threaten the forces of creativity: Is there some power that breaks through into our life to free us from these powerful forces within and around us that are constantly threatening us with destruction?

This question of whether a transcendent dimension to life can be known to us in the midst of life is, of course,

[6] Cox, *op. cit.*, p. 86.

an ancient one; one from which man seems unable to escape. We can illustrate by Immanuel Kant's description of three dimensions to man's self-awareness.

1. *What can I do?* This is the first question native to man's being—the question of his capacity to control nature, and to use his creativity to produce that 'second nature' which is the source of his civilization.

2. *What ought I to do?* Beyond the technological question, man finds himself confronted with the ethical dimension. 'What are the criteria of right action?' 'How can I be responsible to others?' 'How can I be truly human?'

3. *What ought I to hope for?* Beyond the ethical question, man is confronted by the problem of purpose. 'What is life all about?' 'Where does it lead?' 'Can I be free from fate and death?'

Kant's point is that these three dimensions are internal to human existence. They are secular questions about man's life in this world.[7] And here we see one of the great dangers of contemporary secularism—the danger that because of the surging confidence in our productive capacity brought about by the technological revolution, we shall so confine our life to question 1—the technological question—that we will suppress the other questions.

But even if we should admit the second and third questions, we may still conclude that there are no answers: that there is no 'transcendence' in which we can be in touch with 'ethical' and 'religious' realities which abide. We may conclude with a Sartre or a Kafka that the questions of 'ought' and 'hope' simply evoke from us the need to project meaning for ourselves into the vacuum beyond. The death of the old metaphysics results in the dizziness which accompanies the awful freedom of

---

[7] Compare Kierkegaard's analysis of the 'three stages (or spheres) of life'—the aesthetic having to do with man's relation to and enjoyment of things; the ethical; and the religious. Here too Kierkegaard is exploring the dimensions of man's secular awareness.

knowing that we must create ourselves; but this dizziness must not tempt us into contrived answers—as it did in the old cosmological argument for God's existence. As Kierkegaard saw, what that argument means is that man in search for meaning keeps walking back along the chain of causes—on and on. Finally, tired, afraid, dizzy, he sits down. There *has* to be an end. And that 'end' has to be called *God*! But that 'has to' is Freud's 'projection' —a creation of our own needs; a product of concealed despair. And to encourage that type of projection is to ask not only for idols, but for ideologies—for systems that will relieve us of responsibility, and rob us of freedom and creativity. And it is precisely the willingness to let such systems die and to be willing to think from below that is the 'coming of age' of which we have spoken.

Is there then no 'transcendence'—no meaning which transcends time, but which comes to us in time? Is there no truth that holds the open door to ever-new truth? No way that throws light upon our path without restricting our freedom to search for still undiscovered ways? No life that keeps us growing to maturity without reducing our responsibility to seek for ever increasing sources of life beyond those yet known to us?

In his book *The Christian Opportunity*,[8] Denis de Rougemont makes a distinction between two aspects of secularization in the twentieth century : 'the loss of the meaning of the holy, and the loss of the meaning of transcendence.'

The former is marked by the destruction of holiness in public and private life by the process of profanation; brought about by causes such as urbanization, mechanization and democratization, as well as by the popular secularist attitude to life fostered by modern science. The old sacred rituals are being dismantled. Heads of state in democratic societies are no longer ritualistically clothed and consecrated as representatives of the Gods. Wars

[8] Published by Holt, Rinehart and Winston, 1963, pp. 10-12.

are no longer played out within rules suggesting that
they are a drama of God's ordeals and judgments.
Farming, now mechanized, is losing the magical and
symbolic characteristics conferred upon it by the old
religious myths.

This aspect of secularization, de Rougemont concludes,
is probably, on balance, a real blessing. It may have
harmful results in robbing man of a sense of mystery,
but it has the great advantage of eliminating the confusion between natural religion and faith by the elimina-
tion of the former. Similarly it means that men are less
tempted to-day to confuse Christianity with ancestral
religion. Consequently profanation clears the way for
faith by clearing away natural religion.

With the second aspect, however—the loss of a sense
of transcendence—the case is quite different. There it
has brought the shrivelling of man's sense of life. He
believes only in the here and now; and the dimensions of
the beyond are reduced to a point where man himself
is his goal—and even then within a restricted awareness of
the mystery of man himself.

It is here that we must ask what the Christian faith
means by its claim that in a secular event—the life of
Jesus of Nazareth—the meaning of history has come
into the midst of history. In the past, theology has inevitably tried to express the ' transcendence ' of this event
in ' mythical ' or ' metaphysical ' language. The question
now is whether we can discard the mythical and metaphysical clothing in which the Christian faith has been
expressed, and still make sense of the claim that here in
Jesus we are given the transcendent dimensions which
enable us to live creatively within the open secular world
which is itself the fruit of the faith that Jesus evokes.

Tentatively I would like to make an attempt to speak
of three dimensions of the true transcendence which are
given to us in this event of Jesus; seeking to point towards
a language of interpretation which will describe the

significance of the Christian faith to man in the secular age. In doing so we will attempt to point also to the way in which this secular understanding throws light on the mission of the church as the company of those whose task it is to point the world to the way in which Jesus is the meaning of history.

1. *'Eschatological' transcendence (Christ as Lord)*

The Christian faith encounters us with the claim that in the midst of history we are given in Jesus the meaning of history pointing to its goal; or in biblical terms to the eschaton (the end). Its affirmation is that the secular event of the life of Jesus is one which discloses in history the meaning and goal of history. Jesus therefore transcends history because he shows us the end of history.

In the past this claim has often been expressed in mythical and metaphysical language; but now this truth, which centres on a secular event, calls for secular expression. What we are speaking about is an event which took place in a particular historical situation, an event in which the witnesses tell us they encountered in one man a dimension of existence which disclosed to them the meaning and goal of life for all men. In the encounter they discovered in Jesus the true human existence they themselves lacked; through him too they received the hope that this true human existence also could be theirs and that together they could grow up into the true human community in which the full potential of human existence will be realized. The life of Jesus, they discovered, was a life in which the expected limits of human existence constantly were being transcended. In him they met authority, truth, wholeness; through him they were given the assurance of the way and in him they encountered a life which transcended even the boundary of death. They therefore became certain that the life they met in

him was a life which opened up for them the way to
ultimate fulfilment. They became sure of this because
his life was wholly available to them; nothing could
destroy his gracious and forgiving presence with them—
not even their own faithlessness; not even their own final
rejection of him. Even in death—in fact, particularly
in death—his life was given to them and for them.

So it was that they became men of faith projecting their
assurance recklessly into the myths they found around
them. He was Saviour, Lord, ascended one, seated on
the heavenly throne and waiting to come again on the
clouds of heaven. But in such projections of their faith
they witnessed with conviction to the secular discovery
which had come to them in their confrontation with the
man they knew as the Messiah—the final clue to the
purpose of history—the Christ, the Son of God. And our
task now is to do the same, and to project this faith
into the view of our time as they did into myths of
their time.

Let us take an example, from Colossians 3.1-4. It
begins : 'If then you have been raised with Christ, seek
the things that are above where Christ is, seated at the
right hand of God. Set your mind on things that
are above, not on things that are on earth, for you have
died and your life is hid with Christ in God. When
Christ who is our life appears you also will appear
with him in glory.'

The language framework here is mythical-metaphysical :
'where Christ is, seated at the right hand of God.' To
us, also, the consequent advice Paul gives sounds 'religious'
in the sense of withdrawing our attention from this world's
concerns and projecting our lives into a realm that transcends the worldly. 'Set your mind on things that are
above, not on things that are on the earth.' But when
we move on to the verses that follow, this other-worldly
impression is soon destroyed. The 'therefore' which Paul
draws from this mythical-metaphysical Ascension picture

of Christ, takes a surprising turn. He starts off by saying that 'rising with Christ' (sharing in his 'transcendence') requires that we put to death what is 'earthly'; but when he tells us what it means to throw off the 'earthly' ways (which Christ has shown us to be contrary to God's way) we discover that it means accepting *now* a new life *in this world*. This new life is, in fact, the meaning of history that has been disclosed 'in Christ'. 'Here there cannot be Greek and Jew, circumcised and uncircumcised, barbarian and Scythian, slave, freeman, but Christ is all and in all' (Verse 11).

Suddenly the 'transcendent' life is no longer mythical-metaphysical. It takes shape within the very heart of our secular conflicts. The 'earthly' life we put off is a narrow shrivelled worldly life—the life in which we allow ourselves to be restricted by race, religious, cultural and class or caste division. The life 'above' which we put on, is the open worldly life—in which the restrictions to human community are broken through and we enter into that truly human society in which there is full openness to each other. This 'transcendent' life—the life 'above'—turns out to be life which has appeared 'below' in Jesus of Nazareth. In him we have seen, as Bonhoeffer pointed out, the true transcendence of the man who was wholly 'for others'; and who allowed no restricting prejudice or custom to close off his life from that full openness to the neighbour which present society denies but which he has disclosed as history's meaning and goal.

It is an historical vision then that Paul has put into mythical clothes; not unnaturally, for that was normal language in that time, and Paul was taking the language of the day and filling it with historical meaning. But as the centuries went by the mythical-metaphysical language ceased to be the language of everyday life and became instead 'sacred' language. As a result the secular demand of the gospel tended to be lost by an escape from the historical meaning into that metaphysical and religious language of the first century. But all the time the historical vision that Christ had given was hidden within the language and threatening to break through; and now again its secular demand is seeking to break out into the open, though not without deep resistance. And if we are to give this language the meaning given it by Paul in the first century, we must now take off those mythical clothes and put it into the secular context of the world of to-day : the world of race conflict (Greek and Jew), religious hostility (circumcized and uncircumcized), culture clash (barbarian and Scythian) and class division (slave, freeman).

We can see the same 'transcendent' dimension of the meaning of the life of Jesus given by Paul in the Colossians passage, when we turn to the story of Pentecost. There the 'transcendent' dimension of the new life Jesus brought into history now breaks through into the life of the community of his followers. They become the 'eschatological community' in whose life there breaks into history a 'sign' of the life that will at last be given to the total community of man. In their life is seen a 'foretaste' of the final community life of mankind.

To understand the symbolism of the Pentecost story (Acts 2), we must read it as an event in which we are given a reversal of the story of the Tower of Babel (Genesis 11). In that old Genesis story, God is pictured as looking down from heaven with suspicion as men build a tower reaching to the sky. The men are saying : 'Let us build a tower whose top shall reach to the sky.' They want to make God unnecessary by taking over his job and by running the world themselves. God decides that something must be done to prevent the terrible results that would follow such sinful self-assertion, and the action he takes is the same as that taken by the fathers of the American Constitution. Because they believed that sin is too dangerous unless divided; they

divided legislative, executive and judiciary. Similarly God
here in the Tower of Babel story divides sin—he separates
men into nations, with different languages and customs.

But now at Pentecost there appears in the middle of
history an event in which this judgment of Babel is
reversed and in which we see the sign of the final meaning and goal of history. As the disciples come out of
the upper room to the streets of Jerusalem, people are
gathered from all four corners of the Roman world.
As they listen to the disciples they exclaim : ' What does
this mean? We all hear them speak in our tongues the
wonderful works of God.' Now at last Babel is reversed.
Here a community of life is given in which the barriers
of language, custom, race, class are broken down as the
Spirit gathers men of the nations into the life of the
new community revealed in Jesus and now released into
history. Witness to this new life is to be taken ' from
Jerusalem, to Judaea, to Samaria and to the uttermost
parts of the earth ', and so the ' eschatological transcendence' revealed in the life of Jesus becomes the missionary
task of the Church. The Church is given the task of
being in its life the sign of the New Humanity given in
Christ through the Spirit; and the task of witnessing to
this purpose of Christ in the old communities of the world.
It is to show that in Christ there is no ' Greek and Jew,
circumcized and uncircumcized, barbarian and Scythian,
slave, freeman.'

That the church often fails in this mission, often being
the sign of the old age and its divisions rather than the
sign of the new age and its creative unity, is just as
obvious as the fact that it often allows the vision to
become lost in a false metaphysical transcendence so that
its secular meaning fails to break through. But the
vision lives on because Christ continues his hidden work
in history moving on toward the goal he has revealed.
The ' eschatological transcendence' is the transcendence
both of a vision of the end of history given in history

and of a power working toward that end—a power of Christ breaking through from below within the world of secular events.

What this dimension of the transcendence of Christ means for the mission of the church is a question requiring persistent re-examination. Certainly it suggests that the church should be wherever there are conflicts which divide; seeking to be the recipient and sign of this transcendent life of unity and refusing to acquiesce in the lower life of fear and prejudice. 'Put off therefore' the old earthly life with its divisions, and 'put on' the new life of unity in Christ. Refuse to accept those ethnic, caste, cultural and national barriers in which the world seeks to enclose you—whether in housing ghettos, or suburbs, or clubs or nations. Insist on showing your faith in the transcendent life of unity given in Christ as the sign of history's goal; and go to those points of conflict in order to reveal the signs of that new life which gives the clue to the meaning of history.

2. *Grace transcendence* (*Christ as Saviour*)

It follows from what we have said that the transcendence revealed in the secular event of Jesus, is that we see in him not only the life which is the meaning and goal of history; but that we also see in him the one who brings to us in history ' grace '—healing for our lives, and the gifts of truth, love, courage. Here the ' transcendence ' of Christ implies that with a meaning that would be improper for others, he can say to his fellow-men : ' Come unto me.' His transcendence means too, that hearing it, each of us can know that the one who says this to us is the Lord of history who calls me to him, forgives me and commands me. His transcendence for me means that unlike any other neighbour, he is the one who is fully and unreservedly for me, and who is able to draw me into his movement toward the goal he has appointed for us all. He is the one who comes to me in such a way that he discloses my lack of true humanity, my failure to be open to my neighbour and the extent to which I am curved in upon myself; and in doing so he discloses also his grace for me by which he draws me into his new community and trains me in the new way.

It would seem to me that this is the point Rudolf Bultmann—that most radical of demythologizers and secularizers—is trying to make. He has been accused of reducing the Christian faith to only one word—Kerygma, and to one symbol—the cross, by his radical scepticism concerning the extent to which the story has been veiled by myth and metaphysic. This is not really true. He has more left than a Jesus about whom we know nothing for certain except that he died on the Cross and was proclaimed by his disciples as the good news. But though this is not all, to Bultmann it is the key to all. For here in this event of the cross was a secular event in which —according to the disciples' witness (the kerygma)—there occurred a confrontation with the man who was wholly for others, and who revealed to them their own inauthenticity. It was in this naked encounter with the cross that the disciples discovered too the transcendent mystery of grace—' he died for all '. And through their witness the same encounter can take place for me. Here at the one time, I am judged—offered death to the old life; and I am given grace—offered resurrection to the new life of Christ.

Bultmann believes that this is what the story of the resurrection means. Its empty tomb; its varied appearances; its ascension clouds; are projections into the mythology of that time of the miracle of this secular encounter with Christ. And so Bultmann strips the story down (for the majority of theologians he goes too far), but still he points to the dimension of *grace transcendence*; of *Christus pro nobis*—Christ for me.

If the first dimension of transcendence spoke of Jesus as bringing to us within history the awareness that he is the *Lord* of history who gives to us its meaning and goal, this second dimension speaks of Jesus as bringing to us the awareness that he is the *Saviour* of mankind giving to us the true humanity we lack.

3. *Transcendence over death* (*Christ as Pantocrator*)

There is an insistence in the New Testament that one of the reasons the resurrection of Jesus is an event of great meaning to us in history, is precisely because it means that already our life has a centre of gravity beyond the grave. A life is revealed to us in this event which has greater strength and meaning because it is a life that has already 'defeated' death.

Of course this emphasis is subject to misuse. In the pastoral theology of the Middle Ages, for example, they had a section called *Ars Moriendi*—the art of dying—and it was even said that the whole art of life was learning how to die, for life here is simply a short introduction to eternity. The result often was the failure to be open to the 'eschatological transcendence' of which we have spoken—in which this life itself is the scene of movement towards its own goal; the goal of unity in Christ in which we all participate in the New Humanity within a cosmos that has realized its full creative potential under the rulership of man who is appointed as its governor. But yet the misuse of this emphasis on the *Ars Moriendi* does not mean that we should banish it. When we do it always seems to come back again through the rear door—as when a philosopher like Heidegger tells us that the true art of authentic living must be learned in confrontation with death. And when we try to confine the meaning of the transcendence of Christ within a secular transcendence which encloses the secular inside the limits of our contemporary vision (speaking of realization of meaning within history only in the terms we already possess), then our experience of life itself rises in protest.

Kierkegaard, in writing of Hegel's philosophy of history in which the meaning of history finally appears only at the end—the final product of the ' cunning of reason ' working its hidden way until at last the mystery is unveiled—protests against its injustice. Why should all the generations be sacrificed to the benefit of the last one, with only those who are left at the end, when at last the mystery is solved, sharing in the triumph? This ' death transcendence ', revealed in the resurrection of Jesus, proclaims that human life is not e. closed in the limits of this life, but that our life here opens up into a life of fulfilment in which all may participate.

The human existence revealed in history in Jesus of Nazareth, then, reveals not only *eschatological transcendence*—the meaning and goal of history (Christ as Lord); and *grace transcendence*—the giver of true humanity (Christ as Saviour); but also *death transcendence*—the giver of a common life which transcends fate and death (Christ as *Pantocrator*—who finally gathers all things into unity).

In India it is a common sight to see corpses being carried through the streets in open view, down to the river banks where they are burned in public. This is a reminder to the Hindu that while there is death, there is hope of release from this life. For the Christian the life of release from death is already given; already the transcendent life towards which history is moving is taking shape in the life of those who participate in Christ's life. But this life is not fully realized in our present participation in history; and in Christ there is revealed the mystery of a life that transcends the limits of fate and death; and which carries in it promise for all men and for creation : ' Because I live, ye shall live also.'

Kierkegaard has this version of the story of the Wandering Jew. A gravestone was once discovered on which was the inscription 'The most unhappy man'. A search was instituted for the owner. Many came forward with their tragic stories of unhappiness; but still none qualified, until finally the Wandering Jew appeared. 'Is this grave yours?' he was asked. 'Yes,' he replied, 'I'm the most unhappy man. My unhappiness is that I cannot die.' The resurrection gives us the good news of death; the good news that this life begun in Christ ends in Christ. 'If in this life only,' Paul says in I Corinthians 15, 'we have hope in Christ; we are of all men most miserable.' To start living toward that goal of new life in Christ and to get part way without sharing in its fulfilment—that is not our fate. Death is transcended in Christ.

This does not lead us out of history, but into it. In 1964 some Negroes went to celebrate the 300th anniversary of the landing of slaves in the U.S.A. at the site of the first slave market in St. Augustine, Florida. They held a rally proclaiming their right to participate to the full in the Emancipation begun so long ago and not yet complete. Hemmed in by angry whites, they demonstrated in open declaration of their rights, holding a 'wade-in' at the segregated beach, and singing and praying as they walked through the streets to witness to their freedom. The whites threatened them, guns were directed at them; but they marched on. They risked death —and I asked one of the leaders why. His answer was that they believed in the resurrection. And that meant *now*, both because this new life in Christ demands to be shown forth as the life that transcends black and white, barbarian and Scythian, bond and free; and because this new life in Christ cannot be broken by death. Those who die as they participate in the struggle are not left by the roadside by those who walk on to the final goal.

MISSIONARY IMPLICATIONS

It is interesting to notice how Harvey Cox's analysis of the *avant-garde* functions of the church matches quite closely this analysis of the dimensions of 'transcendence' that are present in the secular event of the life of Jesus. This should not be surprising. As we saw ,in the story of Pentecost, the church has the missionary task of carrying forward in history the life revealed in Jesus; or better, its missionary task is to be the vehicle of Christ's continuing presence in history.

Cox speaks of three functions :[9]

1. *The Church's Kerygmatic Function.* The church is the servant of the action of Christ in the world; and to believe the Kerygma means to believe that man is meant to have dominion over the earth and that in Christ the way is open to the defeat of all the powers that hold man back from the attainment of the goal. The church's kerygmatic function is to point to where the action is; and to summon men to a participation with Christ in his struggle against the enslaving powers and his movement towards the goal of history that he has revealed.

2. *The Church's Diakonic Function.* The church has the healing and reconciling task of binding up wounds, bridging chasms, restoring health; and it is called to perform this task by continuing the servant ministry of Christ in the midst of actual conflict, strife and oppression, developing a strategy of mission that will work realistically within the structures of modern urban life in such a way that true healing can occur.

3. *The Church's Koinoniac Function.* The church is to be a fellowship which demonstrates in its life the reality of what it says in its Kerygma and points to in its Diakonia. Its task is to make hope visible; to be a

[9] Cox, *op. cit.*, pp. 127ff.

sign or provisional demonstration of the final purpose revealed in Christ. Drawing on Barth and Ebeling, Cox shows how this functional discussion of the church's work brings the traditional discussion of the 'marks of the church' into a much-needed contemporary framework. Instead of being 'marks' which delineate religious or cultic boundaries and so separate off the church from the world (the classical theologies ran this danger when they defined the church in terms of 'word truly preached', 'sacraments duly administered', 'ministry validly appointed'), these 'marks' describe functions the church performs in and for the world. The church as *avant-garde* has the task of being the point of break-through from the limits of the past on the way to the future fulfilment of Christ's purpose.

Cox is under no illusion that the world is moving, Hegel-like, to the inevitable fulfilment of the hidden purpose that is being woven behind the events of history by the cunning of reason. In the event of Jesus we see the mission leading to the cross; and the mission still goes forward under the sign of the cross. And just as Jesus is presented in the gospels as an exorcist—albeit within the mythical language of that age—so the church must still act as exorcist; but now within the secular understanding provided for us by the social sciences. Cox speaks, for example, of exorcism as 'that process by which the stubborn deposits of town and tribal pasts are scraped from the social consciousness of man and he is freed to face his world matter-of-factly.'[10]

Exorcism means a struggle with the 'principalities and powers' of to-day. These are to be seen in the projected fantasies of contemporary society which take shape in compulsive behaviour patterns; in the variety of forms of prejudice in the inherited power structures which now block the path to a more open society; in the forms of society now holding us back from possessing the promises offered by urban-technological advance. The church's

[10] *Ibid.*, p. 154.

calling is to undertake this exorcist task within the demonic forms of to-day. But the irony is that forms of church life which were fashioned to confront the demonic forms of the tribal and town eras, now often stand in the way of the church's mission. In this way, church forms themselves become demons to be exorcized if the way is to be opened to the future. Cox believes, in fact, that 'the real ecumenical crisis to-day is not between Catholics and Protestants but between traditional and experimental forms of church life.'[11]

This should not surprise us. What we have said of the 'transcendence' of Christ (and therefore of the church's mission) is that Christ reveals in a particular secular event the meaning and goal of history. This means that for us a particular past event becomes the clue to future events; and points us to a continually new task if we are to be faithful to the vision. But the temptation always is to give that past event a wrong form of transcendence by lifting the past event (or some past witness to it) out of history, so making it static and safe. The result is that we face a need for continuing reformation. The reformation involves not just the problem of being open for what Christ is doing now in history so that we may allow the church to perform its *avant-garde* functions; it also involves the task of breaking out of the forms which threaten to enslave the church in the past. The Roman Catholic theologian Hans Küng has reminded us of the danger that just when the Roman Catholic Church seems to be learning the truth of the Reformation slogan, *ecclesia semper reformanda* (the church always being re-formed), the Protestant churches may be retreating from the essential truth their motto contains. That would be tragic irony; but if the whole church is to move out on the road to reformation, it is important that we should be searching together for the right path.

[11] *Ibid.*, p. 160.

THE RIGHT WAY TO REFORMATION?

The problem of how to move creatively away from the forms of the past and how to read the signs of Christ's presence in the world of our time is now a major question that faces all of us. The Roman Catholic theologian Joseph Ratzinger states one facet of this problem suggestively. The way to reformation, he insists, is at the same time a backward and forward movement, for the transcendence of Christ means that we must go both backward to him and forward to him:[12]

On the one hand the church 'is based entirely on a fact of the past, namely, the life, death and resurrection of Jesus Christ which the church proclaims on the basis of the witness of the apostles as the salvation of men and the source of eternal life. . . . The obligatory norm of renewal can only come about by a new orientation from its origin. . . . Mere concessions to the times or mere " modernization " are always false renewal.'

On the other hand ' although the renewal of the church can come only from turning to its origin, it must be something altogether different from restoration. . . . This is so because the historical Christ . . . is at the same time the coming Christ in whom the church hopes. . . .

'As the faith of the Old Testament has a two-fold orientation in terms of time : one toward the past, namely, the miracle of the Red Sea by which Israel was saved from the Egyptians and which was the founding of its existence as the people of God; and one forward, toward the days of the Messiah in which the promises made to Abraham would be fulfilled; so the historical existence of the church has two poles : it is referred back to its founding in the death and resurrection of the Lord, and forward to his Second Coming when he will fulfil his

[12] *The Church and Mankind, op. cit.,* pp. 65-6.

promise of making of the world a new heaven and a new earth.'

In traditional language this points to a major question: how can we be open to the Christ leading us into the future? How can we discern the signs of his presence in the events of our time calling us to new forms of presence? The theological development we have been following forces us to the kind of statement made by the Executive Secretary of the Youth Department of the World Council of Churches, Albert H. van den Heuvel:[18]

'The discovery that the church is not the only tool God can or does use to work in his world but is rather the announcer and celebrator of his work, has not yet been fully digested, but has attracted the attention of many, especially younger theologians. It has made them scouts for the footprints of the Master in the world, who conceive their primary task as discerning where signs of God's presence in the world can be seen, so that they may indeed celebrate them, point them out, and try to be faithful to them.'

It should not be assumed however that this looking for the signs of Christ's footprints as he leads us into the future, is an attitude which has attracted favourable attention from all the major theological minds of our time. On the contrary; Karl Barth, as we have seen, has viewed it with strong suspicion. Barth warns against the tendency of man to say 'Lo here', 'Lo there' and to project his own ideological desires into history, declaring that in them he discerns the presence of God. Barth's primary word in connection with our attempts to discern in events the signs of God's presence, is a word of judgment against man's inveterate tendency to stamp his own self-interest with the seal of God's approval. It is in this light that we must understand his well known warning

[18] In the WCC Youth Department Bulletin, 'Complex Society: Structures of a Missionary Church', no. 10, November 1964, p. 21.

against the tendency in the U.S.A. to identify her cause
with God's future; and his insistence that the Eastern
Communist lands probably pose less of a threat to the
future than the U.S.A. The reason for the distinction
lies in his insistence upon the danger of idolatry in
the United States' identification of God's presence in their
values, as against the fact that the communists make no
such claim to identification with God's cause.

Barth's hesitation over all attempts to make a positive
identification as to what God is doing in history, and
his concentration upon the 'otherness' of God and his
judgment upon our pretensions, can easily be understood. The existence of this danger was all too apparent
when Barth began to write. When World War I came,
there were preachers a plenty on both sides of the
conflict who traced with confidence the marks of Christ's
footsteps in the cause for which they fought. On the
British side they proclaimed that the war against Germany was a holy crusade for the victory of a truly human
way of life, developed under the impact of the gospel,
over the forces of paganism rising up in apocalyptic
opposition to the gospel's progress. But at the same time,
German preachers with equal confidence justified the
German cause in the same terms. No wonder then,
that the post-war Barth should raise his word of warning
against all such tendencies to say 'Lo here', 'Lo there'.

But is Barth's warning enough? Bonhoeffer believed
not. He believed that at this point Barth was too much
a prisoner of neo-Kantian transcendentalism. It is here
that he criticized the 'positivism of revelation' in Barth.
To fail to develop alternative and Christologically sound
criteria for how we are to act in history in response to
God's purpose, only opens the way to unexamined judgments. We must obey the command of Christ to read
the signs of the times; but we are required to heed the
warning in several of his parables that we must be
open for the surprising claims of God pressing in upon us

through our neighbours (see, e.g., Matt. 25). The problem, then, is one of developing criteria to aid us in the search for the footprints of Christ. What then are some of these criteria?

This attempt to give three general criteria is quite tentative; and it should be stressed that the order is important. To jump to 3 before 1 and 2 would be to invite danger. In 1 and 2 are given the precautions needed to prevent over-enthusiastic or over-optimistic reading of the presence of Christ in the world.

1. Barth himself has pointed to one criterion. The tendency to project our own self-interest upon history and to assume it to be the will of God is an inevitable concomitant of our human sinfulness. The prophets' emphasis upon the judgment of God; their warning that judgment must begin in the house of God; the warnings of Christ that his claims will break through with surprise; all these should make it clear that we must view our own identifications with suspicion and be prepared to see in them the institutionalized expressions of our original sin.

This inveterate tendency to believe that our ' way of life ' is obviously the best way to health for all can be illustrated from a prevalent attitude in the church at John Wesley's time. In many of the sermons of the age we see real concern for the lower classes; but it is assumed that if the working classes are to be saved and are to enter into Christ's purpose for them, then they must take on the culture of their betters who stand as a living sign to these outcasts of what happens to our raw, untamed, animal nature with all its sins (i.e., working class life) when the grace of God tames it and begins to fulfil it (i.e., the life of the better classes). In other words, it was assumed that the will of God was to make ' them ' like ' us '. Probably it was because Wesley (like Jesus himself) went to these people not to make them like their betters, but to enable them to find the way of Christ for them in their own world, that he was so bitterly attacked. His missionary presence with the lower classes was a judgment upon the ideological assumption of the privileged and so threatened the security of their own prejudices which they assumed to be the will of God.

This warning criterion given us by Barth then, is a Christological criterion. In the way Christ moves out to the world, we see a freedom for the 'other' which stands in judgment against the tendency of the religious better people of the time to assume that the way of salvation for the outcast was for 'them' to become like 'us'. They assumed that they could see the signs of God's presence in their own way of life and revealed an amazing capacity to project their own way of life on to their world as a means of determining what God was doing.

The first criterion then is one of 'judgment' against our tendency to 'ideological projection'. The significance of this for our attempts to find the appropriate forms of missionary presence in our day is far-reaching. We see in the 18th century church attitude in Wesleyan England exactly the same process in operation as we observed in the British and German churches in 1914. We see it to-day in a wide variety of situations: integration means 'them' becoming like 'us'; peace means their acceptance of our value system; independence requires that they first rise to our standards of behaviour so that they will not threaten our civilization.

2. This leads to a second criterion—a positive one. We must see the world and what Christ is doing in it in the light of the cross before we attempt to see it in the light of the resurrection. To put it in Luther's terms, we must operate with a *theologia crucis* (a theology of the cross), not with a *theologia gloriae* (a theology of glory). British and German preachers operated with a theology of glory, each seeing the *parousia* (the final coming of Christ) in their own cause. But our first question must not be one in which we ask how we are to be the vehicles of

the Parousia—such utopianism is denied us, for we struggle only for signs pointing to the End; the End is not within our reach. Our first question must instead be one of how we can be witnesses to the crucified servant Lord. Our task is to be with him in the midst of the world's needs, by his grace seeking to be the signs of his ultimate fulfilment, not the bringers of that fulfilment.

This means that we see our missionary task under the sign of the cross; we see that the way of mission is the servant way in which we are freed from conformity to the world's self-assertive ways and transformed to the way Christ assumed in his ministry for us.[14]

9. The third criterion is less easy to state. It has to do with seeking the signs both of Christ's presence and of resistance to his presence within the key struggles that are taking place in the events of our time. It is concerned with looking for the signs of new hope and new life that Christ is bringing to birth, and for the forms of resistance to these hopes. Let me illustrate from the book by the French Roman Catholics, Louis and André Rétif : *The Church's Mission in The World.*[15] The Rétifs make an attempt at reading the signs of Christ's presence in the world by looking at the 'values' which they see appearing where previously they have been absent—truly human values struggling for existence in contemporary societies. In values such as modern man's concern for freedom, his concern for others, his dream of 'a new city', his longing for life freed from despair, they see 'presentiments of the salvation whose Alpha and Omega is Christ.' They see in these emerging hopes and in the new discoveries opening the way to the

---

[14] In *Where In The World?*, chapter 1, pp. 24ff., I have a major section on 'The Shape of the Mission: The Servant Method'.

[15] A volume in 'The Twentieth Century Encyclopedia of Catholicism', edited by Daniel Rops, Hawthorne, New York, 1962, especially pp. 36ff.

wider fulfilment of these hopes, the signs of Christ's
hidden presence. Consequently they see them also as
signs calling for missionary presence : as 'points of
insertion for the seeds of the gospel !' They quote with
approval Cardinal Suhard : 'The discoveries which are
being made with increasing rapidity should not be for
the Christian a mere item of news or no more than
scientific tidbits. They have a genuine value as signs
and they must be integrated into the Christian's apostolic
vision of the Redemption. They are not just adding orna-
ments to the existing universe, they are building a new one.
And it is this new universe and no other that we are
called to serve.'

There is danger here in this search for 'values' : danger
of imposing our own values, rather than those suggested
by the vision of the goal of history given us in Christ.
The Rétifs are aware of this; they know too that the
form in which such values appear will be a mixture of
true and false hopes, and that when Christ is working
his hidden ways, so also are the demonic powers. That
is why they conclude : 'The mission of the church as
regards values . . . is to make it possible for them to
be rediscovered in the light of God. . . . It is for the
Christian to bear witness within the values the modern
world contains, and to live by them while at the same
time transcending them; but he must also witness to
the values the modern world forgets.'

The process of testing these values must be one of
continuing dialogue between the hopes and values rising
in the world, and the various symbol projections given
in the New Testament of the hope introduced by Christ.
There we see the visions of a new heaven and a new
earth, of the City of God, of the New Humanity in
Christ in which all divisions are overcome, of the kingdom
without temple (and presumably without clergy), of a
cosmos with its full creative potential realized. There we
see the description of the way to the goal—with its life

for others, its servant identification with the needs of men, its faith in the ultimate victory of self-giving love. And it is through an insistent dialogue between those biblical symbols and the new hopes and struggles of our time, that we must seek the discovery of the forms of missionary presence that Christ is calling forth from us in the world of to-day.[16]

In seeking to express this understanding of the forms of Christian presence required of us to-day, we will need to know our world by all the skills of knowledge that it provides. We must be open to it; know its heart-throbs. Then we must seek to etch in for our day symbols that will suggest the shape of the missionary obedience that is called forth from us in our urban society—in the same way that the eschatological symbols served that function in the New Testament day; and in the same way as the symbol of the 'City of God' served in Augustine's day[17] or symbols such as the 'priesthood of all believers' served those of Reformation times;[18] or the symbol of new-born converts revitalized the church in Pietist days.[19]

It is here that we see the significance of a work such as Gibson Winter's *The New Creation as Metropolis*[20] with its attempt to give the vision of the New Humanity

[16] The development of 'coffee shops' and other forms of 'dialogue presence' in various parts of our culture—among youth, artists, scientists, etc.—is a recognition of the need to relate the eschatological symbols of the biblical tradition to the various symbol worlds of to-day, waiting for the mysterious 'strike' to occur in which the tradition comes to life in the symbols of our time.

[17] See the *City of God*, Augustine's famous book.

[18] In Reformation times the description of the 'two realms', sacred and secular, and of the 'orders' within which the laity were to exercise their priestly obedience—family, labour, government and church—provided a satisfying framework in which large numbers of the laity were able to visualize their daily lives.

[19] See below, chapter iv, p. 115.

[20] Macmillan, New York, 1963.

contemporary form in the midst of urban-technological society. By this concrete spelling out of the vision, his aim is to enable us to hear the call of Christ summoning us to serve the needs of the contemporary neighbour in the midst of the urban culture of to-day. What he is doing is to engage in this dialogue between the biblical eschatological symbols and the present hopes and aims of urban life, and out of the encounter to fashion a living symbol which will serve to give us a vivid picture which will draw out our missionary obedience to the work Christ is seeking to accomplish in our society.

This is what van Leeuwen is attempting when he seeks to give the outlines of a 'philosophy of history' for to-day; not in a system of Hegel's type, but in an open reading of the historical events of to-day which accepts responsibility in the light of what God has done in the past for interpreting the direction of what he is doing at present.[21]

That is what Harvey Cox is seeking to do in his attempt to move to a 'political theology',[22] in which theology accepts the responsibility for being ' that reflection-in-action by which the church finds out what this politician-God is up to, and moves in to work along with him. In the epoch of the secular city, politics replaces metaphysics as the language of theology', because it is now politics (in the broad sense of the science of the polis) which does what metaphysics once did—it brings unity and meaning to human life and thought.

In all such attempts then to read the signs of the times, to see the shape of God's action in the events of the day, we see the essential form of our search for forms of missionary presence. It is inevitable that we will be impatient; inevitable that church people will press the ' how ' problem, asking for the answer to the question : how should the church be organized and what are the

[21] See below, chapter iv, pp. 118-21.
[22] Cox, *op. cit.*, pp. 254ff.

proper techniques of evangelism to-day? This 'how' question has its proper and essential place. But its place is in the midst of this dialogue with the world; we cannot know the 'how' ahead of time. Its place is in the midst of experiments with new forms of presence.[23] The 'how' question must be kept a living question in the midst of a 'pilgrim theology' that keeps looking for the moving presence of Christ, and the question of technique must be kept subject to the continuing revision that comes from constant experimentation.

Another problem with the 'how' or 'technique' question to-day is the way in which it has become so tenaciously associated in our minds with the world's standards of success. Time and again, as we face the need for allowing the methods of the last generation to be replaced by new forms of obedience, we find ourselves thinking that if we can only find the right and relevant method we will soon be as successful as they were. We assume that we are meant to be; and that faithfulness and good judgment will bring their rewards in visible attainment. In a most suggestive article on 'God's Arithmetic',[24] Hans-Ruedi Weber challenges this assumption. He analyses the biblical evidence to show that 'evangelism and outward church growth will not necessarily go together.' In fact, Paul's apostolic joy was based not on outward success, but on the opportunity to share in the sufferings of Christ through witness and service (martyrdom). And the essential growth was growth in maturity —commitment to God's kingdom and his righteousness.

If this is really what God's arithmetic is like, many things must be changed in our traditional under-

[23] I have outlined some of these in chapter iv of *What In The World?* In the Study of 'The Missionary Structure of the Congregation', the search has led inevitably to experimentation. What is needed, however, is not imitation of experiments, but participation in the concern leading to the acceptance of widening responsibility for experimentation.

[24] An unpublished mimeographed address.

standing of mission and missionary methods, and we must be converted to the biblical criterion of maturity instead of trying to become or remain a majority church, or bewailing the fact that nowadays we are increasingly a minority. This does not necessarily imply a condemnation of every *corpus Christianum,* because it may well happen that, at a given time and place, God elects, calls and converts a majority to be his people. It is not very important whether the number of Christians at a particular time and place is large or small. What is much more important is the question whether the large or small number of Christians know that they are there as representatives for all and that they are called to participate in the mission of the reconciliation of the universe. We must leave it to God whether and when he wants to use our worship and witness in order to add to or cut down the number of his militant church on earth. The Western churches must free themselves from their assumption that the *corpus Christianum* is the norm, and the minority church living in diaspora the exception. On the other hand, small minority churches in the East must be freed from a ghetto-mentality which assumes that God is only concerned with the few and not also with all nations, religions and revolutionary movements. We may pray for the numerical growth of small Christian minorities and rejoice if new members are added. We must also pray for the renewal of large Christian majorities and not panic when God answers our prayer by cutting down our number. Church history would seem to suggest that growth in maturity often fosters numerical growth in minority church situations, while in majority situations it often brings about a healthy diminution of church membership, because many nominal Christians discover that true discipleship is costly discipleship and makes demands which only a few are prepared to accept. A minority church can recognize God's reconciliation mission in the world and serve it whole-heartedly just as well as a majority church. Each has its own temptations, weaknesses and possibilities. It may be that God always provides a provisional homeland for the church, a *corpus Christianum* on which the world-wide Christian diaspora can fall back and which can be its basis for mission. Yet it seems more likely that in our age of universal history, with its world-wide secularization, all Christians are called to live in the world as a minority. This need not be our concern.

This is not the whole story, however. Dr. Weber's point is that the effectiveness of witness is not to be measured by majority or minority status; for whether there be few or many in the church, the church does not exist for itself. It exists for the world, as the part for the whole (*pars pro toto*).

' " Church-directed ministries " are not ends in themselves; they are given to the church for its decisively important " world directed ministry " of reconciliation. Therefore in election God's salvation is not restricted but, on the contrary, presented to the whole world.'

In the last chapter now we turn to the direct questions of evangelism; and in doing so we will speak more of the situation of evangelism than of its methods.

CHAPTER FOUR

EVANGELISM IN OUR DAY

We have spoken of the widespread awareness that we are in the midst of a major crisis in the relation of the church to the world—an awareness cutting across all the denominations and making it apparent that the biggest danger of division in the churches now is not *between* denominations, but *in* all denominations. It is the split between those who are seeking to move out into the world as the arena of mission, discovering the unity which is God's will for us in the act of responding to the call of God coming to us from the midst of the events of to-day, and those who see the first need as the maintenance of the 'given' form of the church coming to us out of the past. The former group asserts its loyalty to the latter emphasis; but believes that loyalty to the 'past' Christ is maintained only by being open to him as he comes to us out of the future. The latter group in its turn asserts its loyalty to the need for being open to new forms of responsibility; but insists that Christ is 'the same yesterday, to-day and forever' and that therefore his gifts—of Word, sacraments, dogma, ministry—are 'without repentance'.

In the stimulating article, 'Toward A Secular Understanding of The Ecumenical',[1] Albert van den Heuvel sees the emergence of a new approach to the ecumenical task. It is one which will build on the results of the earlier approaches: the *Erasmian* tradition which encouraged the search for unity by acting upon the basis

[1] WCC Youth Department Bulletin, *op. cit.*, particularly pp. 21-2.

of the minimal agreements already reached, the individual or Pietist understanding of the ecumenical which stressed the need for a common personal commitment as the basis for united witness, and the *churchly* understanding which insisted that true unity requires the full meeting of our divided traditions so that the wholeness of the body of Christ can be restored. Accepting the vital contributions of these three former approaches, says van den Heuvel, we must move on to the next stage. He believes, in fact, that already we are entering this new phase, and that we are moving into a period in which we are learning to seek unity in the midst of a common commitment to the world. 'The interest of many theologians has switched from the interest in a churchly understanding of the ecumenical to a secular one, of which the main characteristic is a search for ways in which the actual degree of common understanding and basic unity can function in provisional (not claiming to be the ultimate answer), vicarious (on behalf of the whole divided church) experiments of service and unity in the world.'

The heart of this *secular* understanding does not lie in despair over the possibility of theological agreement by internal church discussion—although it must be said that there is a relative despair over this old approach which sought union along the path of inner-churchly dialogue. Nor is the heart of this secular understanding to be found in the pragmatic judgment that if the churches work together on common tasks many of the old fears and suspicions and many of the ' non-theological factors '[2] that divide us will fade away—although it should be said that this insight is strongly affirmed. But the heart of the secular understanding is deeper than either of these insights. It lies in the positive conviction that the path

[2] ' Non-theological factors ' seems to be a euphemistic name for the forms of ecclesiastical pride and prejudice which we are not willing to list under the appropriate theological category—original sin.

to unity lies along the way of common secular involvement;
for the simple reason that the world is the true addressee
of Christ's concern, the true object and stage of God's
active love, and the place where he is at work. It is
for this reason that it is affirmed that it is in the midst
of worldly commitment that we are meant to receive the
light we need on the path to unity and renewal. This
theological conviction also carries with it the knowledge
that it is not just any kind of common worldly commitment that will do. It must be a common commitment to,
and at the same time a search for, the presence of Christ
in the world. It is a commitment in which as separate
denominations we confess that the true sin of our division
is that we are no longer truly available to Christ for
his reconciling work in which he seeks to lead the world
to true unity. It is a commitment in which we are
prepared to be drawn out of our denominational dis-
unities by seeking common servant tasks in the midst
of the secular world; believing that if we allow God
to address us at the point of our common search for
true obedience we will receive the further light we need
on the path to unity—a unity which is, after all, not
for our own sake, but for the sake of the world.

There is no escaping the fact, however, that while
there is real pressure at present in the direction of
this movement of the church towards the world—a pressure
cutting across all our former lines of separation—there
is also a strong resistance to this approach, a resistance
too which cuts across all denominational lines. The resistance roots in the fear that this movement out to
the world, particularly before we resolve our theological
differences or before we reach deeper levels of internal
spiritual depth, can only result in the pouring out of the
Christian faith upon the desert sands of the secular
world. This crisis within the church, concerning the
relation of the church to the world, is deep; perhaps

as deep (and as promising) as that which confronted the church at the time of Constantine or at the time of Luther.

The conviction of those who are pressing towards a major re-shaping of the relation of the church to the world can perhaps be summarized by pointing to three levels of change which they believe to be necessary— changes, also, which they believe to be already occurring.

First, they believe we are in the midst of *a massive restatement of the gospel,* with the need for the discovery of a new language of interpretation in order that we may fulfil our missionary task. This we have called the problem of 'mental structures'.

Second, they are sure that we are on the threshold of *a major realignment of the forms of the church's life;* spurred by the necessity of discovering new forms of Christian presence in the world if we are to fulfil our missionary calling. This we have spoken of as the problem of 'institutional structures'.

Third, they speak of the necessity we are facing for fashioning *a new Christian style of life,* centring upon the necessity of discovering ways in which the laity can discover their secular ministries—learning to live within the structures of urban technological society in such a way that they can fulfil their missionary task of witnessing to the shape of the kingdom of God as it breaks in upon the kingdom of this world. This problem we may describe as the search for 'personal and community structures'.

That changes are already occurring in all three of these levels of the church's relation to the world is clear. They are changes that are ignoring the old confessional lines, and (not without strong resistance—again a resistance that is 'ecumenical'!) are affecting all our denominations equally; no doubt for the simple reason that we live in the same world and are subject to the same revolutionary forces. Some of the characteristics of these changes would seem to be:

1. *A new climate of openness to the world.* Take, for example, the title given by the World Council of Churches to their 1966 conference on church and society—'World Conference on Church and Society : Christian Response to Social and Technological Revolution'. Or take the slogan that has gone the theological rounds in recent days to the effect that we must 'let the world write the agenda for the churches' mission'—that we must discover what are the shapes of the obedience that is being called forth from us, by the process of learning to discern the new shapes of need and the new structures of hope that are emerging in the fast-changing patterns of the human communities of to-day.

Of course, an objection occurs immediately. Why should the church's mission be one of *response* to the world's changes? Is not the church meant to hold the initiative because she represents the God who has taken the initiative? Is she not commissioned to go to the world, calling the world to respond—'Repent and believe the good news'? Why then should the church let the world write the agenda? Is not the agenda of mission written in unchangeable characters across the face of history—JESUS CHRIST, the same, yesterday, to-day and forever?

Yes : this affirmation is essential. But the very reason why this emphasis on openness to the world has arisen —the reason why this openness to the claims presented by the world's agenda has broken into the centre of the search for the shape of the church's mission—is precisely that the church is learning again to turn its eyes to Christ. It is he who is the same yesterday, to-day and forever (not the church); and he is the living one. And it is in him that this openness to the world is seen. This is what it means to say that his coming was a secular event. This is what it means to speak of his 'transcendence' as coming from below. He revealed in history the meaning and end of history, and for that reason is the same yesterday, to-day and forever. But he is the same not because he is untouched by our time, but because he is always and unchangeably involved in the events of our time. It is he who emptied himself of all claims to timelessness and freely delivered himself up for us all—opening himself to our needs—even though that openness led to the death of the cross. It is he who in his supreme openness to the needs of the world took upon himself the form of a servant. He was the one who broke free from the ghetto of religious law and cultic regularity in which the faith of the time was so largely imprisoned, in order to be free for the needs of the outcast, the hopeless, the helpless. And it was he who warned those whom he called to share his mission to the world, that they too must be free for the unexpected need by the roadside; and that true greatness is in the willingness to be the servant of all. Rightly understood therefore, openness to the world—readiness to read the world's agenda as a call to missionary response—is itself a witness to the changeless mission of Christ.

It is, of course, true that our response to the world's agenda is not to be dictated by the world's expectations. Christ emptied himself; but not in such a way that he became a reed shaken by the wind. He emptied himself of all but love; but it is in that redeeming love that his mission is given. And we too in witness to him are envoys of that servant love—and therefore in our openness to the world, witnesses to a redeeming presence for the world.

Again it is true that when we read the agenda of the world, we can interpret it correctly only in the light of Christ. But in turn we are learning that this light of Christ comes to us only when we are ready to move out into the midst of the world—only when we leave the safe boundaries of the temple and the law where we so often try to keep God imprisoned, and are open for the light of Christ coming to us from the strange worlds of our neighbours. So often it is this unexpected light

from Christ which enables us to read the world's agenda:
'When did we see thee hungry and feed thee, or thirsty
and give thee drink? And when did we see thee a stranger
and welcome thee?' And it is as this unexpected light of
Christ comes to us through the world's agenda, that we
are offered freedom from the smallness of vision and the
limited obedience that continually threaten to strangle
the church's mission. And it is this freedom that we need
—the freedom for Christ as he comes to us from the
world of which he is Lord; freedom to be with Christ
as he moves on in his missionary pilgrimage toward the
goal of history. As he moves on toward that goal, he
continually summons his church to the tasks of pointing
to his presence and of joining him where the action is.
And he warns his church that they can be free to be his
witnesses only if there is in us a constant readiness for
surprise: 'Watch therefore, you never know when he
will appear.'

In this first characteristic of the changing relation of
the church to the world—openness to changing shapes of
need and to new forms of hope—we can quickly see the
reason why there is to-day a radical re-examination of the
forms of our missionary obedience. Let me illustrate by
just one example.

In Latin America the churches to-day are facing a major
crisis brought on by a major transformation that is occurring in the attitude of the masses. After centuries of
mass despair in which the vast majority assumed that
there was for them no hope of meaningful participation
in the benefits of life in this world, there is now taking
place what can only be described as a ' secular conversion '
—a turning from secular despair to secular hope; from
resignation under injustice to a determination to build a
society where all men will have a new dignity and a
freer participation in a more truly human community. For
the churches the question is: how is this ' secular conversion ' to be treated? Is this a sign of Christ's presence,

calling the churches into the struggle for this new hope?
During the period of mass despair the Protestant churches
have said to the people—and properly—'In the world
there is for you despair and exclusion; but in the
community of the church you will receive the acceptance
the world refuses you, the dignity the world denies you,
and the spiritual guidance and community that will be
for you a foretaste of that life in the kingdom of God
for which you were created.' But now, in the emerging
new situation of secular hope, what are the churches
to say? Is this now a call from Christ to the church
to turn its life out into the mainstream of the world's
struggle? Is this a call which says 'In the years of your
despair, I called you out from the world to fashion
for myself a people who know my grace and are formed
by love; but now the hour has struck for you to see the
signs of new hope that I am giving to my people in the
world; and to join me in the midst of the struggle,
interpreting that hope, struggling to keep it free, and
helping the people to know me as their Lord and Saviour
in the midst of the events of their daily life '?[3]

Here in this one example, then, we can begin to see how
openness to the world can carry with it radical changes
in the forms of our missionary obedience.[4]

2. This brings us to the second characteristic of the developing changes on the edge of the church's relation
to the world; and this is the *recognition that the vast
changes brought about by the rise of urban-technological
society are calling forth* from the churches *new shapes of
missionary obedience,* to an extent that is threatening to
shatter some of the inherited shapes of the churches'

[3] For documentation of the changing situation in Latin America,
see *What In The World?*, pp. 31ff.

[4] The significance of this, e.g., in terms of the relation of
the churches in the U.S.A. to the 'mission' the government
is assuming in Latin America, is clearly far-reaching.

theological thinking, the churches' formulation of ethics, and the churches' institutional life.

A listing of some of the characteristics of this urban-technological revolution will make clear something of the implications they carry for the life of our churches. I will mention three :

First, the vast increase in the *power of man to master the world* is for the first time making it possible for the masses to share in a creative life in this world. For the first time it is becoming possible for the masses to eat enough to lead a truly human life, and to learn enough to free their life from imprisonment in the immediate moment so that they can become responsible members of the human race and free participants in history. So also for the first time it is becoming possible for those oppressed because of race, or of nation, or of caste, to gain enough power to break the chains of oppression and participate now in the worlds of politics and culture.

Second, this vast upsurge of *freedom for life in this world* is bringing with it the death of old religions, old metaphysical systems, old theologies. Man is becoming secular man—concerned to understand life from within and to master life from below.

Third, this great increase in control over environment is bringing too, the *new shape of urban life*—life where men are no longer associated on the basis of tribe, or ethnic group, or national difference; but where men must either learn the secret of openness to all men as neighbours, or else destroy themselves in resisting that openness which is the logic of urban-technological mobility.

These and other characteristics of the urban-technological revolution are pregnant with missionary implications for the church. Do we not see in the new mobility with its pressure toward openness, the pressure of God breaking down dividing walls of race, nationality, caste? Do we not see in the fearful resistance to these movements, demons to be exorcized in the name of Christ? Do we not

see in the costly struggle to overcome these demons of
prejudice and fear, the need to witness to the costly
love of the cross? Do we not see in the rising freedom of
the masses, a movement toward the fulfilment of God's
promise and commandment to man that he will subdue
the earth? Do we not see in the breaking of the age-long
chains of oppression, a movement toward the promise that
mankind shall grow up into one new man in Christ—into
a unity in which all the dividing walls are at last broken
down? Do we not see in the resistance—even the terror
—that accompanies these changes a call for the church
to move into the midst of these changes, witnessing in
word and life to the true hope revealed in Christ and
sharing in the costly struggle for the victory of these hopes?
Can we not see in the collapse of old religious systems,
old metaphysical certainties, old theological constructions,
and in the rise of newly confident secular thinking, a
call to us to speak in witness to Christ as the one who
came in human form, the one who came to set man free
from old systems of thought: free to know God in
the immediacy of human life; free to serve God in the
world of the secular? Can we see in this the possibility of
what is being called a 'non-religious interpretation of
the Christian faith'—in which, through our witness, Christ
again is revealed to man, not in the hidden mysteries of
a strange theology, but as the one who came to set the
oppressed free and who makes himself known in the
events to which we can point:

'Go and tell what you have seen and heard—the blind
receive their sight, the lame walk, lepers are cleansed and
the deaf hear, the dead are raised up; the poor have
good news preached to them' (Luke 7.22).

It is at this point that we can understand the emphases
that have emerged in the World Council of Churches' study
on the Missionary Structure of the Congregation. The
basic theme of that study is that the church as institution must be understood as the servant of Christ's con-

tinuing mission in the world; or to put the basic theme
in another way : that the ' marks of the church ' (Word,
sacraments, godly fellowship) are not to be understood
statically, as changeless forms in which God comes to man
in a religious realm outside the ordinary affairs of life.
Instead the marks of the church must be understood dyn-
amically.[5]

(a) The church *is*, where *preaching* is pointing to
what God is doing in the world—where we are witnessing to Christ's continuing redeeming work and calling
for disciples to join Christ in his redeeming work.

(b) The church *is* where *sacraments* are a re-enactment
—or perhaps better, a celebration—of the drama of God's
redeeming work in Christ, which enables us to see through
the once-for-all drama, to the continuing presence of
Christ in the drama of history to-day.

(3) The church *is* where the *fellowship* of the church
reveals to a world afraid of the pressure of God towards
an open community, that in Christ there is no Negro
or white, no European or Asian, no high caste or low
—for in Christ God's purpose to make us all one finds
its fulfilment.

So the Missionary Structure of the Congregation study
has been exploring ways by which the church can now
be freed for this mission—freed for God's work in the
new worlds of our time; for Christian presence in the
new shapes of human existence in the structures of our
time.

In this context we can understand the crucial significance of the way our churches are struggling to find
new ways which will enable us to respond creatively
to such major crises as those which have emerged in the
areas of race, poverty, changed patterns of family life,
new patterns of urban decision-making. We can under-

---

[5] See chapter III, p. 90 above, where reference is made to the
replacement of these traditional ' marks ' in the writings of
men like Ebeling by ' functional marks '.

stand why it is said that the true shapes the church must
assume to-day are the shapes of servant presence around the
new forms of human need and hope.

But there is *one problem* in all this that is *causing deep
worry in the churches*. The worry is expressed in various
ways; but the variety of expression points to a common
concern. Are our churches now too concerned about
social problems and too little about conversion? Are
they too involved in politics and secular affairs, and too
little engaged in the central task of the church—evangelism and spiritual life?

The reason for this question should be clear: it lies
in the realization that a major change is occurring in
the missionary strategy of our churches and there is
an uneasy feeling that by widening our concern to the
circumferences of life, we are in danger of vacating the
central emphasis upon the one thing needful—the emphasis upon the need to call sinners to repentance and
to new life in Christ.

There is no doubt that we are here at the nub of it all.
Why is there this drastic change in missionary strategy
to-day? Why is pietism now denigrated? Why is appeal to
individual conversion not kept unwaveringly at the centre?

The answer here must be sought in the changed historical situation in which we find ourselves. It is easy
for us to forget that the evangelism with which most
of us are familiar is itself the outcome of a quite drastic
revolution in missionary strategy. It came in the 18th
and 19th centuries. It came in Europe and in the
U.S.A. through Pietism and the Evangelical Awakening.
And it came because sensitive Christians became aware that
something was seriously wrong in Christendom. Søren
Kierkegaard put it this way: ' Is it possible for man to
become a Christian in Christendom?' Gradually it had
become the assumption that everybody in Europe or
America—with the exception of the few infidels—were
Christians by birth. And as Søren Kierkegaard said, all

that was needed to remain a Christian was a little water
at baptism, a little rice at marriage and a little earth at
death. But the tragic result was that because it was
assumed that people were Christian and the culture
was Christian, the need for appropriating the faith and
for becoming aware of its demands and open to its promises—the need, in short, for learning to die with Christ
to the old life of the world in order to rise with Christ
to the new life in the kingdom of God—this need was
lost. Consequently a missionary strategy was developed :
a strategy of concentrating upon the moment of decision;
of calling upon the hearer to become what he already
believed himself to be; and to appropriate the truth which
he already assumed to be the truth of his life.

The development of this new evangelical strategy was
one of the great moments of Christian history. From it
new life broke forth from the old Christendom : new
freedom for Christ that streamed out into the mission
fields, the new lay movements, and the new social concerns of that time. But now we are in a new situation.
Let me mention just two factors.

i. We do not live in Christendom : where the Christian
tradition is assumed to be true; where the masses believe
themselves to be Christians. We live instead in a world
where vast new powerful secular forces are sweeping across
our world bringing the incredible changes to which we
have already referred. And we must ask : What does
it mean to-day to call people to Christ? Has it not become
clear now that to call them to conversion; to call them
to accept Christ as Saviour without helping them to see
the nature of the changed life that is required by Christ
as Lord, is in fact one of the grave dangers for the
church to-day?

So, for example, for us to ask men to be disciples of
Christ without enabling them to see how Christ is at work
in the race revolution, and for us to call men to conversion without enabling them to see how Christ calls

us all to repent of our prejudices and to be open to the fullness of life in which there is no black nor white, is to practise an evangelism that can be in fact false witness—a religious escape from Christ's demands.

ii. This links with the second factor. In the 18th and 19th centuries where the older pattern of evangelism was forged, the more individual patterns of village life made it easier for individuals to grasp immediately the responsibilities of the life of discipleship. But the rise of the complicated patterns of urban society makes it increasingly important that the new forms of evangelism to-day should enable the call of Christ to come to the bearer in such a way as to enable him to count the cost of discipleship within the structures of his secular life.

An example of the change from the individualist pattern of village life to complicated patterns of human existence in cities is provided by the vastly different forms the lives of the 'outcasts' have now assumed. In the village these needs had names; the village alcoholic was known; the problem people were known. If the church in the village had any sensitivity to its mission, it was able to reach out to such people and draw them directly within the ministry of the life of the parish. But now with the rise of the city, the shapes of outcast life have undergone vast changes. Needs for the most part no longer have names; the alcoholics, the drug addicts, the homosexuals, gravitate together into communities of anonymity, and the rejected minorities crowd together in separate worlds of ghetto rejection. The result is that now our residential congregations no longer 'see' their responsibility of ministry to the outcast individuals, and the evangelism that takes place inside the communities of our congregations—communities from which these needs are by and large excluded—no longer is able to point its converts to the missionary responsibilities involved in discipleship. For the convert to understand this, he must be helped to see the new shapes of need, and he must be helped to search for new forms of church life which will reveal his responsibility within these worlds of need.[6]

What we are called to to-day then is an evangelism in which calls for decisions for Christ (and these we must make) are related to calls for decisions ' in Christ ' : to a call to be free for the presence with Christ within the struggles of our time where Christ is working to overcome prejudice and poverty and political irresponsibility and international tribalism in order that all men may grow up together as one new man in Christ.

In the work to which we have referred[7] Arend van Leeuwen seeks to spell out the need for what he calls a ' comprehensive evangelism '—the equivalent of the slogan familiar in ecumenical circles : ' the whole gospel for the whole world '. Van Leeuwen is convinced that our evangelism to-day will fail in its purpose unless we can enable contemporary man to understand what God is doing in the events of our time, and unless we enable him (in the light of the revelation given in Christ) to discover his own place in God's unfolding purpose for history. Thus, for example, we must help contemporary man to see that it is out of the Christian vision of the unity of mankind—a vision given in such passages as : ' it is the purpose of God in the fullness of the ages to gather up all things in heaven and earth alike into unity in Christ '—that there has been born the concept of International Law and the idea of the United Nations. As Christians we are called to provide a prophetic inter-

[6] See *What In The World?*, pp. 73ff., for suggestions of ways in which the church may find appropriate forms of presence in these worlds of need. But again it must be stressed that we are only beginning the exploration of the new forms that are needed.

[7] *Christianity in World History*, *op. cit.* In stating his position in the next few pages, I have taken the liberty of developing it in my own language and in an expanded form. His statement I found to be fragmentary and not easy to follow. In rewriting it, I hope I have been faithful to the intention of a statement that seems to me to be of first-rate importance.

pretation of the events of our time, showing how such
events call us to a struggle too against the powerful forces
standing in the way of the realization of that purpose.
True evangelism, in fact, requires us to witness to God's
purpose for the nations and to call men to turn to God
and to accept his purpose for their lives.

But to do this, the call must be translated into the
vital practical affairs of our day. As an example, van
Leeuwen calls for the abandonment of the term ' assistance
to underdeveloped countries '. In practice that still speaks
of the ' white man's burden ', and of relations of superior-
ity and inferiority; and thus it fails to witness to the
purpose of God revealed in Christ—a life of unity in
which all men will belong to one family; all living equally
by his free grace.

In terms of this present situation in this planetary
world of ours, we are required to see the fantastic in-
equalities of welfare between different peoples and nations
as a persistent danger to the peace which God intends
for his family, and therefore as a call to Christian involvement and obedience. The very existence of such vast
economic contrasts can only mean that such a society
lives on the perpetual verge of revolution. As representa-
tive of the purpose of Christ to bring peace to his
people, the Christian will see himself called to involvement in the struggle to do away with these contrasts; but
he will see his involvement not in terms of superiors
coming to the aid of inferior people, but as brothers
sharing with brothers the one grace of our Lord Jesus
Christ—a grace expressed in all the capacities of the
creation which he has given to us all richly to enjoy.
He sees the problem therefore as a mutual problem for us
all, calling for a gigantic effort of all mankind to move
together under God's creation command to ' subdue the
earth ', and under the redemption promise of Christ
that the unity of mankind in mutual responsibility shall
finally be given to us. For this reason then a much better

slogan than 'economic assistance to underdeveloped
countries', would be a slogan such as 'economic demo-
cracy for the world'.

This is but one concrete example of the major problem
that lies behind it. This major problem, van Leeuwen
believes, is the problem of witnessing within these particular events to God's purpose for history: and it is the
failure to do this which represents the true dimension
of the present missionary or evangelistic crisis. As the new
countries of Africa and Asia leave their old 'ontocratic'
societies and enter the new 'technocratic' world, they are
undergoing a radical change in the traditional structure of
their life. The forces bringing this change from the old
sacral societies to the new secular community have emerged
from the Western 'Christian' world. But the irony is
that the 'free West'—that is, the traditionally Christian
Western nations—now has separated the technical assistance it is giving these new nations from a discussion of
the question of what the emergence of the new society
means. The Communist countries, on the other hand,
carry in with the technical assistance a new ideology
purporting to explain the collapse of the old sacral
societies and what the next stage of history will be.

The result is that while the Christian faith has been
the underlying force leading to the changes in Asia and
Africa that are breaking down the ontocratic age and
opening the way to the technocratic society, the nations
in the West from whom these forces came now are failing
in the task of enabling these nations to understand the
events in the light of the Christian faith. As a result,
we have left a vacuum for the false ideology to enter—
and then we wonder why our much larger technical
assistance is not leading the new nations to join our side
of the Cold War (as though that should be our major
concern!).

What van Leeuwen calls for is an evangelistic or
missionary approach that accepts responsibility for de-

veloping a 'philosophy of history'—not in the sense of
giving a total framework in which every event can be
placed; but in the more immediate sense of interpreting
our present developments in the light of Christ's on-going
purpose for history; and of seeking to state the policies
we develop within the light of this continuing attempt to
see what Christ is doing within the events of our time.
This missionary task is urgent not only for Asia and
Africa : it is a universal task. It is as important to understand the race crisis or the schools crisis in the U.S.A.
in this light, as it is to understand the situation in Viet
Nam. In fact the common root to both crises is a discovery
urgently requiring our attention.

The crisis in mission is a world-wide one; it is the
crisis in our interpretation of what God is doing in history.
It is a crisis which we have been attempting to explore
throughout these pages within the rubric of the rise of
the secular society. And what is being suggested is that
' evangelism '—calling people to a knowledge of Christ as
Saviour and Lord—depends in the first place upon the
understanding of what God is doing in our history, and
how he is calling us to join Christ in his action in the
world.

In our day, however, the recognition of this ' secular '
development does face the church with a serious temptation. It is the temptation to forget that the need to
see Christ working within the variety of struggles in our
time, carries also with it the need to see Christ as the
one calling us to repent (to die to our selfish ways) and
to be converted (rising again to new life with him, as
we learn to be free to serve our neighbour). In other words,
the danger is that we shall forget the evangelistic task
of the church as the framework in which we must see our
service of the world.

In our day, evangelism is needed as the breathing spirit
throughout the wide-ranging and changing forms of the
church's missionary responsibility. We may need to be

reminded that decisions for Christ in the wide range of human problems to-day must not be separated from the decision for Christ that must be the continuing centre of the life of every disciple. But similarly in our day evangelism needs as its essential context the wide struggle of the church to discern the work of Christ in the world of our time; for only in this way can evangelism be delivered from falsely separating individual decisions for Christ from the continuing decisions to which individual Christians are called within the structures of our common life. Evangelism, in other words, must include both the pointing to the presence of Christ as Lord in the affairs of our world and the pointing to the call of Christ as Saviour of each of us; for then we see that Christ calls each of us to abandon our false worldly ways—our petty tribalisms, our limiting sectionalisms, as well as our personal selfishness—and to accept his grace in such a way that as forgiven sinners we will be enabled to live as servants of his kingdom within the kingdoms of this world.

Evangelism needs to be placed in the midst of the struggle to discover the new shapes of Christian obedience within the human communities of our time—in inner cities, in town and country; in the decision-making structures; in the worlds of international affairs, of politics, mass communications, leisure and the rest. In this way it is affirmed that the call to decision for Christ should be related to the ways of obedience that now must be fashioned in order that the church may be present with Christ in the communities of the world, raising the signs of the coming kingdom.

* *This note to page 42 was included by the author at proof stage. (Publishers):*

There are 'theologians' who want to go further and who speak of the death of God as not only the death of older metaphysical ideas of God or the death of psychological apprehensions of God. They speak of the death of God as an 'historical event'. (William Hamilton, Thomas Altizer.) It is not easy to grasp their meaning. One statement on this level that I think I can understand is that of Albert Camus. For him the proclamation of the death of God was a cry of anguish, leading him to accuse the world itself of being Absurd. His objection to the organized religion of our time is that it offers to introduce us to God; but when we accept the invitation we discover that all that is left at the Royal Court is the protocol. The King is not there at the introduction. Camus' 'atheism' is truly 'theology'—a word about God. Its agony is the absent God. Even in his absence God is inescapable. But when Hamilton and Altizer speak of the death of God as 'good news' I can only believe that they are misled by an unfortunate confusion. The death of outmoded metaphysical and psychological ideas of God is good (though deeply painful) for it opens the way for the true knowledge of God for which we wait (though often with feelings of despair). But to speak of God's death as an historical event, as though the whole God idea is now left in the past, is to suggest that man can never again be claimed by One who is the meaning, end and guide of history.

INDEX OF BIBLICAL REFERENCES

Gen. 11	82	Acts 2	82
Exod. 20.2ff	37	1 Cor. 15	88
Matt. 25	95	11 Cor. 4.7	17
Mark 10.43	65n	Col. 1.23	8
Luke 7.22	113	3.1-4	80
John 14.12	32	3.11	81

GENERAL INDEX

Abraham, 37, 92

Abrahamic motif, 36

adulthood of the world: Christian attack upon, 58; need of respect for, 61

Africa: church and, 14; development in, 120f

aggiornamento, 14

Alabama, 45

American Constitution, 66, 82

anti-Christ, kingdom of, 31

Apostles, the, 62

Ars Moriendi, 86

Asia: church and, 14; development in, 120f

Augustine, St., 99

autonomous man, 59

Bacon, Roger, 43

Barth, Karl, 46, 47ff, 90, 93ff

Bethge, Eberhard, 54, 60f

Bible: modern reading of, 23f; story continued in history, 32

Biblical faith: in the functional era, 23ff; 32f; secularisation the fruit of, 26ff; and religion, 47

Body of Christ, 49

Boman, T., 34n

Bonhoeffer, Dietrich, 41, 46, 47, 54ff, 61n, 63, 81, 94

Bultman, Rudolph, 56, 85

Byzantine court ritual, and liturgy, 10

Christ: as Lord of the world, 9, 31-2, 79ff, 110, 122; his coming a secular event, 51, 73; the meaning of history, 79, 84, 87; ' eschatological ' transcendence (as Lord), 79ff; grace transcendence (as Saviour), 84ff; transcendence over death (as Pantocrator), 86ff; his presence, 94ff, 110

Christendom: development, 30; position of church, 66, 72; breakdown, 64ff, 116

Christian culture: and two realm theory, 63; renewal of, 70ff

Christian faith, and theology, 44

Christian ' presence ' 12f

Christian task, the, freedom and, 72

Christianity: growth, 30; to-day, 62ff

church, the: reform, 7, 91; primitive, 8-9; past structural changes, 9ff; loss of institutional control over world,

125

church, the: (cont.)
20, 29, 38, 43; its servant role, 66, 97, 113-14; its missionary task, 83, 98; Diakonic function, 89; Kerygmatic function, 89; Koinoniac function, 89-90; as avant-garde, 90*f*; two poles of historical existence, 92-3; crises in its relation to world, 104*ff*; the three marks of, 114

circumcision, and salvation, 55
city, period of, 23*ff*
Commandment, the First, 48
Communism, 70*ff*
Constantine: time of, state adoption of church, 9*f*; after, 37
Corpus Christianum, 102*f*
Cox, Harvey, 24*ff*, 38*f*, 49*ff*, 89*ff*
creativity: and nihilism, 33, 73; openness to, 71
cross, the world and the, 96-7
cultic practices, 47, 51

Death of God, 41*f*
death transcendence of Christ, *see* Christ
desacralisation, 26, 39*n*
Deus ex machina, 55, 61
discipleship, 102-3, 117
disciplineship, 56

Ebeling, Gerhard, 61*f*, 90
ecclesia semper reformanda, 91
ecumenical, *see* unity
Eliot, T. S., 70-1
Enlightenment, the 21
Erasmian tradition, 104
eschatological transcendence of Christ, *see* Christ
Evangelical Awakening, 115
evangelism: techniques of, 101*ff*; and spiritual life, 115; comprehensive, 118*ff*

faber suiipsus, man as, 68
faith: opposed to religion, 47*ff*; *see* also biblical faith
feudalism, 10*ff*
Florida, Negro demonstration in, 88
Foucauld, Charles de, 12*n*
freedom, for Christ, 110
Freud, 74, 77
functional period, 22*ff*
functional thinking, 26

Gannon, Professor Joseph, 43*f*
God: relation of Jews to, 23*f*, 29*f*, 39*n*; in history, 29*ff*, 38, 50; is free, 39*n*; his transcendence, 50-1; is secular, 59; our understanding of, 59; his ' arithmetic ' 101-2
gospel, restatement of, 107
grace transcendence of Christ, *see* Christ
Greek view of life, 34*ff*; contrasted with Hebrew, 35*ff*

Hebrew-Christian view of life, 35, 37*f*
Hegel, 90, 100
Henry, Carl F. H., 62*n*
Hindu, and death, 87
Hitler, 63
Hitlerism, 57

ideologies, 77
idolatry: in relation to the religious, 48, 52; as secularism, 53

Jaspers, Carl, 21
Jesus: his secularity, 51; in our lives, 61; as exorcist, 90; *see* also Christ
John xxiii, Pope, 14
Judaeo-Christian tradition, and the technocratic society, 29
Jung, Carl, 41

Kafka, 76
Kant, Immanuel, 40, 76
Kerygma, the, 85
Kierkegaard, Sören, 17, 76n, 77
Küng Hans, 91

Latin America, churches in,
  110-11
Law International, 118
Leenhardt, 36
liberalism, 56
love, in witness, 109
Luther, 18, 96

Margull, Hans Jochen, 13n
materialism, 71
Messianic age, the, 27, 92
metaphysics: meaning, 40;
  physics no longer dependent
  upon, 42; is religion, 60;
  secular withdrawn from, 64;
  replaced by politics, 100
'Missionary Structure of the
  Congregation,' 12ff, 10n,
  113-14
monasticism, 10
Mosaic motif, 36
Munby, Denis, 71-2
myth, period of, 21-2

Nazism, 70
Neolithic revolution, 28
New Humanity, the, 98-9
New York Times, the, 43-4
Nietzsche, F., 41, 74

Ockenga, Harold John, 62n
oikumene, meaning, 30
ontocratic era, 28ff
ontological period, 22f
open society, the, 66f, 72ff,
  108ff
Open, von, 67
Orthodox churches, 11
otherness of God, 47, 94

parish system, the, 97

Parousia, the, 96-7
Paul, St., 8, 51n, 101
Pentecost, and eschatology, 82ff
'philosophy of history,' the,
  121
Pietism, 115
profanation, 77-8
Protestant churches, the, and
  reformation, 91

Rahner, Karl, 68n
Ratzinger, Joseph, 92-3
Reeb, James, 45f
Redemption, vision of, 98
Red Sea, miracle of, 92
Reformation times, 99
religion: in the secular age,
  33; critique of, 47f; and
  faith, 47ff; and salvation,
  55; *deus ex machina* concept and, 60; is individualism, 60; is metaphysics, 60;
  collapse of, 112f
religiosity: in the Sabbath, 48;
  and metaphysics, 50-1, 54ff

sacraments, 51n, 90
saeculum, meaning, 34
salvation, St. Paul and, 51n;
  'presentiments' of, 97
Sartre, J-P, 76
Satan, seeds of, 31
science: in light of biblical
  faith, 32; and religion, 40
Schillebeeckx, 68n
Schweizer, Eduard, 9n
scripture; Barth's view of, 48;
  new theology and, 68
secular attitude, 26, 33, 46
secular conversion, 110f
secularisation, fruit of the Incarnation, 57f
Second Coming, the, 92-3
Sinai covenant, as deconsecration of values, 39
Spirit, the, 69, 83
Suhard, Cardinal, 98

systems, old metaphysical, death of, 112*f*

technocratic era: 28*ff*; as outcome of Judaeo-Christian tradition, 29
technopolis, *see* city, period of
Ten Commandments, purpose of, 37
tension, in Old Testament, 36; with way of world, 56
theocracy, Jewish, 29*f*
theology: in middle ages, 40; as 'reflection,' 44*f*; liberal, 56; new, 68*f*; political, 100; death of old, 112*f*
'thinking from below,' 39*ff*
Thomas Aquinas, St., 44
Tower of Babel, 82*f*
town, period of the, 24*ff*
transcendence: loss of meaning of, 77; in Jesus, 78; wrong form of, 91; *see* also Christ and God
transcendentalism, neo-Kantian, 94
tribe, period of the, 24*ff*
truth, Hebrew understanding of, 24
two realms theory, 62

United States, 94, 121

unity: secular approach to, 104*ff*; Erasmian tradition and, 104-5; individual understanding of, 105; churchly understanding of, 105
urban technological revolution, some characteristics of, 112*ff*

van Buren, Paul, 47
van den Heuvel, 93, 104*f*
van Leeuwen, Arend Th., 28*ff*, 38, 49, 52*ff*, 118*ff*
van Peursen, Cornelius, 21*ff*, 38, 49
Viet Nam, 121

Weber, Hans-Reudi, 19, 101*ff*
Weizaker, von, 29, 32
Wesley, John, 95-6
West, Charles, 43
'What in the World?', 15*ff*, 101*n*, 111*n*
'Where in the World?', 14*ff*
Winter, Gibson, 99*f*
witness, and suffering, 9
world, as arena of mission, 104*ff*
worldliness, 57
World Council of Churches, 12*ff*

Yahweh, 39*n*